The Prairie School in Iowa

The Prairie School in Iowa

RICHARD GUY WILSON

SIDNEY K. ROBINSON

The Iowa State University Press / Ames / 1977

RICHARD GUY WILSON is assistant professor of architecture, University of Virginia

SIDNEY K. ROBINSON is assistant professor in the Design Center, Iowa State University

Illustrations in front matter: ii, Louis Sullivan (Burnham Architectural Library, Chicago Art Institute); iii, Frank Lloyd Wright (Library of Congress); iv, detail of Sullivan ornament; viii, detail of Wright ornament.

Photograph credits: Unless otherwise noted, photographs from authors. Page 44, William Wagner; 48, 49, Architectural Record, 1912; 51, Western Architect, 1914; 65, Alfred Caldwell; 66, 67, Western Architect, 1924; 69, Architectural Record, 1916; 70, Northwestern University; 83, Western Architect, 1911; 92, Architectural Record, 1914; 112, 113, American Architect, 1919; 114, Architectural Record, 1924; 122, 123, Western Architect, 1921; 126, Western Architect, 1914; 127, Western Architect, 1912.

Composed and printed by The Iowa State University Press

First edition, 1977

Library of Congress Cataloging in Publication Data

Wilson, Richard Guy, 1940–
    The Prairie School in Iowa.

    Includes bibliographical references.
    1. Prairie School (Architecture) 2. Architecture—Iowa. 3. Architecture, Modern—20th century—Iowa. 4. Wright, Frank Lloyd, 1867–1959. 5. Sullivan, Louis Henri, 1856–1924. I. Robinson, Sidney K., 1943– joint author. II. Title.
NA730.I8W54   720′.9777   77-2788
ISBN 0–8138–0915–0

Contents

Preface

THE CONCEPT for this book arose during the assembling of "The Prairie Style in Iowa," an exhibition supported by a grant from the Iowa Arts Council, assisted by the Department of Architecture and the Design Center, Iowa State University.

The book is connected thematically with the exhibition but we have attempted to provide a more thorough and critical study.

Grateful acknowledgment is made to the many people who contributed. First and foremost we must mention the owners of the buildings who, when we asked, opened their doors and shared the special delights of Prairie School architecture with us.

With the exception of the Woodbury County Court House all the buildings catalogued are private property and the privacy of the occupants should be respected at all times.

Many other people have contributed to this work: staffs of local libraries who answered our numerous inquiries, our colleagues, and our students.

Special recognition is owed to certain persons who contributed significantly: William Chilton, Brian Johnson, Wesley Shank, and Steven Stimmel.

Numerous original drawings and photographs were supplied by the Art History Department of Northwestern University, the Northwest Architectural Archives of the University of Minnesota, and the Burnham Architectural Library, Art Institute, Chicago.

Finally, we would be remiss if we did not acknowledge other students of the Prairie School on whose work we are building: H. Allen Brooks, Norris Kelly Smith, Dr. Robert McCoy, W. R. Hasbrouck, Henry Russell-Hitchcock, and Leonard K. Eaton. While the work has been shared equally, Richard Wilson was largely responsible for the first essay and Sidney Robinson for the second.

Certainly not every Prairie School building in the state has been discovered, and we hope more will be recognized as a result of this study. Much research remains to be done with the buildings and their architects as well as other aspects of the Prairie School. For the most part, the Prairie School buildings are understood and thoughtfully preserved by their owners. Still, several others face the prospect of being drastically altered or destroyed, and the intent of this study is to alert the citizens of Iowa to a unique and irreplaceable aspect of their heritage. Moreover, it is true that the concepts of the Prairie School are not merely historical but do have application today.

Introduction

"T H O R O U G H L Y saturated with the spirit of the prairie," is how Frank Lloyd Wright described his work in 1903.[1] Nestled in the broad flat landscape of the Midwest are buildings that are part of the region, that belong. In the history of art and architecture, regional styles have been one of the more creative and fascinating attempts by people to project their own identities. The Prairie School style of the midwestern United States is one example, founded very directly on the climate, land forms, and life-style of the region. Its uniqueness is unquestioned; the buildings by Frank Lloyd Wright, Louis Sullivan, and their followers are recognized as important contributions to contemporary architecture and art. Beginning in the Chicago suburbs and small prairie towns, the Prairie School has influenced developments worldwide from the Netherlands to Australia.

Chronologically the Prairie School has two distinct and separate periods. The first was in the Chicago area in the latter 1890s. It spread across the Midwest and ultimately to other parts of the country and overseas in the first two decades of the twentiety century, finally ceasing in the late 1920s. After a hiatus, Frank Lloyd Wright, who had removed himself from the scene in 1909, returned in the mid-1930s with renewed creative energy. The second period is more national in scope, with Wright designing buildings from California to New Hampshire, but still the Midwest was his focus.

Within the Prairie School in both periods, a wide latitude in personal expression was achieved by the individual artists, yet overall they remained largely faithful to certain principles. The buildings are abstractions of midwestern landforms and nature, simple geometrical forms enlivened by special ornament; thistle flowers on the flat prairie. Flat or gently pitched roofs and low proportions echo the silhouette of the landscape. Environmentally appropriate, the buildings are designed with elevations oriented for natural ventilation and heat and with deep overhangs shielding against sun and snow. The buildings are intended to occupy a middle range between jarring obtrusiveness and submission to Rousseauian primitivism. They are part of the landscape but still apart: images of human patterns and organization. Materials range from brick and wood, terra-cotta and stucco, to steel and concrete, but characteristically, they are used naturally. Seldom used are highly polished marbles, shiny metals, intricately carved woods, and fine-cut ashlar of the high style architecture of the East Coast and Europe. Inside, the Prairie School building is opened up with the number of compartments diminished and combined, creating a life-enhancing space. The Prairie School architects broke away from the established canons of architectural style and created a different expression of architectural form and spatial experience.

Iowa has always had a special relationship to the Prairie School. Its citizens early appreciated and commissioned Prairie School buildings, and in more recent years again supported its precepts. In such cities and rural towns as Sioux City, Mason City, and Grinnell some of the most important examples of Prairie School work can be found. Equally as significant, though, is the variety of Prairie School work across the state in places large and small—Des Moines, Clear Lake, and Newton—that constitutes a unique heritage of modern architecture.

The Prairie School in Iowa

The Early

BACKGROUND

Historically, the origins of the Prairie Style are tied to the emergence of the Midwest to national social and economic importance in the latter half of the nineteenth century. Chicago, the financial and cultural center of the region, grew phenomenally both in population and economic output. The impact of this expansion was felt in a number of areas: suburbs, transportation, and architecture. A new building type was needed for the business district and the Chicago architects created what is called the Chicago Style: large commercial buildings with a maximal amount of floor space on a minimal ground plot that could be adapted to a variety of uses: department stores, offices, apartments, warehouses, and hotels.[1] This Chicago commercial style had a variety of expressions but in general it forcefully stated the method of construction (the structural frame); avoided imitating foreign styles of architecture; and often reached heights of ten stories or more.

LOUIS SULLIVAN (1856-1924)

Of the architects involved in the establishment of this style, one of the most important in giving this expression to the skyscraper was Louis Sullivan (1856-1924). Sullivan's contribution was two-fold. First, he was a superior designer and he brought out the essence of the building's program through revealing the frames and a new style of naturalistic ornament. Secondly, he was a philosopher brooding on the relation of architecture to civilization and especially to a democratic society.[2] Between the years 1879-1895, Sullivan, in conjunction with his partner, Dankmar Adler, produced a variety of buildings in Chicago and throughout the Midwest that confirmed his talents. But then Adler left the partnership and Sullivan's natural arrogance and inability to compromise combined with a propensity to alcoholism started him on a downhill slide. Within the Chicago commercial idiom, a change became apparent. Revived historical styles were used to clothe a commercial structure as in the Fleming Building in Des Moines and the National Bank in Cedar Rapids, both 1909, by the prominent Chicago firm of D. H. Burnham and Company (Fig. 1). From 1900 to his death in 1924, Sullivan was spurned by Chicago financiers and developers, and reduced to designing small banks and stores in dry, dusty farming towns of

2

Prairie School, 1900-1930

Ohio, Minnesota, Wisconsin, and Iowa. Also during these years Sullivan wrote more than before, asserting the relation of form to function and architecture to society, "I say that a certain function, aspirant democracy, is seeking a certain form of expression, democratic architecture—and will surely find it . . ."[3] His adopted position as a critic of the establishment brought him a following among younger architects, and gives him the role, in spite of his small number of designs, as a spiritual leader of the Prairie School.

Fig. 1. Des Moines, Iowa. Fleming Building, D. H. Burnham and Company, 1909.

Frank Lloyd Wright (1867-1959) worked for Sullivan between the years 1887-1893 until a disagreement caused him to leave and open his own office.[4] In contrast to the commercial buildings of Sullivan, the vast majority of Wright's commissions were for suburban homes and while he maintained an office in Chicago, the majority of his work was carried out at his suburban Oak Park home and studio. In the years after 1893 Wright experimented with a variety of styles while moving towards his characteristic expression which fully emerged by the year 1900. Typical of Wright's fully developed style is the Ward W. Willets house, Highland Park, Illinois, 1902, with low proportions; outstretching form; wide eaves; walls treated as flat thin membranes; structure delineated by trim; the free flow of space on the interior between the dining, living, and entry areas and a focus on the fireplace (Fig. 2). Between 1900 and 1909 Wright completed about 120 commissions largely located in the Midwest. In this he was assisted by the staff he gathered around him in his Oak Park studio; such people as Marion Mahony, Walter Burley Griffin, Barry Byrne, and William Drummond, all of whom we will meet again later. Wright was the central figure in creating this regional style of architecture. However, he was a part of the larger group we call the Prairie School. For not only was it Wright and his staff who were designing with similar aims at the turn of the century but a number of other Chicago area architects as well.[5]

*Fig. 2. Highland Park, Illinois. Ward W. Willets house, Frank Lloyd Wright, 1901–1902, Marion Mahony, delineator (*Ausgeführte Bauten und Entwürfe von Frank Lloyd Wright, *1910).*

Aspects of this parallel development can be seen in two Iowa buildings. The demolished Sedgwick S. Brinsmaid house on Grand Avenue in Des Moines was designed in the years 1899-1900 by Arthur Heun (1869-1946) of Chicago[6] (Fig. 3). Heun belonged to an informal mealtime club, the "Eighteen," consisting of architects of similar sympathies, including Wright. Composed around a cross axial plan, the Brinsmaid house was more com-

Fig. 3. Des Moines, Iowa. Sedgwick S. Brinsmaid house, demolished 1971, Arthur Heun, 1899–1900 (Chicago Architectural Club, Catalogue of Exhibits, *1902).*

partmentalized with less spatial flow than Wright houses of the same period. Flat wooden trim and geometrically patterned leaded glass on the interior bore a strong resemblance to Wright's work. On the exterior Heun adopted stylistic features that in time will be identified as Prairie School: a rectilinear geometrical form, banded windows, light-colored stucco walls, and a thin, low, gable roof. The unusual flip to the gable ends is oriental and similar to the Japanese character of many of Wright's work from this period.[7] Less dynamic than Wright's forms, Heun's design is still within the Prairie School idiom. Also in this form is the First Church of Christ, Scientist, Marshalltown, Iowa, 1902-1903, designed by Hugh Garden (1873-1961)[8] (Cat. 25). Garden was also a member of the Chicago "Eighteen," and perhaps a closer acquaintance of Wright's than Heun. The First Church of Christ, Scientist, is designed on a Greek cross plan, topped by a steeply pitched roof. Resting on masonry foundations, the walls are wood framed with a smooth stucco finish and a slight batter. Large windows in the side gables are divided by vertical mullions and filled with greenish-yellow opalescent glass. Window and door trim is made of narrow raised bands of wood on the stucco wall surface. In contrast to the exterior, the interior is disappointing with a semi-Medieval basketry of exposed struts. Garden's church has characteristics similar to Wright's work, and while the steep roof appears to be distinctive, Wright had previously used such forms.[9]

5

While the Prairie School was a personal creation of Wright and other architects of the turn-of-the century period, it also reflects broader cultural concerns and influences that should be considered. On an international scale it was a regional manifestation of the revolution in the arts that took place around 1900 in locations as diverse as Vienna, Brussels, Glasgow, and Paris. Locally, it was spawned in part by the Chicago Commercial School and its investigation of alternative styles and programs of architecture. However, the Chicago School concerned itself only with commercial buildings and not a style applicable to all buildings as did the Prairie School.[10]

ESTHETIC SOURCES

On an esthetic level, the Prairie School was one answer to a long quest by American architects for an identifiable American style. A constant debate of the nineteenth century had been the question of the uniqueness of the American character, and its manifestations in art, music, and literature. Architecture was a special problem, and in these years countless varieties of styles were introduced as "the American style." Arguing that all history was the province of the new nation, foreign historical styles had ruled the day. The Prairie Style was a specific manifestation of this concern. Regional in its development, it broke free of East Coast and foreign models of taste and style. While designed specifically for a region, it could be built anywhere, and in time was. In a sense the striving for an American style was the main theme of much of Wright and Sullivan's work.[11]

Regional in its concerns, the Prairie School did still draw upon other architectural developments. One was the creation on the East Coast of the shingle covered house in the 1870s and 1880s. Combining motifs drawn from the seventeenth-century American wooden vernacular and the British Queen Anne, these houses had open interiors visible on the exterior through a thin envelope of wall and window openings. Designed by such architects as McKim, Mead and White, and Bruce Price, the shingle style houses had an influence on the Prairie Style; but by the mid-1890s they were considered passé by their creators.[12] Eclecticism so present in American architecture of the period was also present in the Prairie School. But it was more an interest in exotic and primitive sources, Japanese architecture as already noted, or Pre-Columbian architecture which manifested itself in both massing and ornamental details (Fig. 1 and Cat. 19, 27). Also influential was the ubiquitous vernacular housing of the Midwest: square prismatic boxes, interior volumes expressed by a balloon frame covered in clapboards, a porch across the front, and minimal ornament (Fig. 4). These vernacular types provided Wright and his followers with arrangements of volumetric massing that can be seen in his designs such as "A Fireproof House for $5,000" (Fig. 5). Wright opened the interior and gave it horizontal proportions through roof, trim, and windows arranged in banks.

Another major source for the esthetic of the Prairie School was the Arts and Crafts movement. Originating in England with William Morris, who emphasized the moral quality

6

Fig. 4. (above) Ames, Iowa. Residence, Duff Avenue, ca. 1900.
Fig. 5. "A Fireproof House for $5,000," Frank Lloyd Wright, 1906, Marion Mahony, delineator (Ladies' Home Journal, April, 1907).

of handicraft design, it was explicitly a reaction to the industrial revolution. In the United States the movement was less social, though invariably good design was a precept to the improvement of society. Chicago was one of the important centers of the Arts and Crafts movement and the Prairie School one of the unique manifestations.[13] However, importantly, Wright felt the reliance on handicraft outmoded for the twentieth century and called for the "Art and Craft of the Machine."[14]

Tangential to the Prairie School were several other derivations of the Arts and Crafts movement that should be noted, for example, Gustav Stickley (1858–1942) and his *Craftsman Magazine* (1901–1916).[15] While Stickley ignored the Prairie School except for publishing one of Sullivan's bank designs and a few of his essays, there was a familial tie between his mission furniture and interiors and those of the Prairie School (Fig. 6 and Cat. 38). Stickley, along with others, promoted the bungalow house that rose in popularity in the period, 1895–1925. Between the bungalow and the Prairie School there was a cross fertilization of ideas and forms: open plans, unassuming scale, direct treatment of materials, and low horizontal proportions. Some writers felt the Prairie School house was simply a regional variation of the bungalow, "in keeping with the flat plains of the Central West."[16] Homemaker and shelter magazines of the period were also important in popularizing the Arts and Crafts movement. The *Ladies' Home Journal* and *House Beautiful* not only published Wright's and other Prairie School architects' works, but also ran a series of articles that explained how to construct houses with Prairie School characteristics (Fig. 5).[17]

*Fig. 6. Craftsman home number 8 (*Craftsman Magazine, *June, 1906).*

CULTURAL IMPLICATIONS

In a social sense, the Prairie School style was not calling for a reorganization of society, but it did have some important cultural implications. During the turn-of-the-century period, the United States was undergoing a thorough social upheaval. New methods of work and labor, consumerism, transportation, and communication were placing increasing pressures on the American family as a nuclear unit. The home as an institution was crumbling and Wright in particular responded, as several historians have convincingly asserted, by studying the objectives of family life and using this analysis to form the basis of his designs.[18] In Wright's houses family life was paramount, the emphasis was on the fireplace, the dining room, and areas combined for family activities. Much of this interest

8

of Wright's in the dissolving family came from his own unsettled childhood in a broken home, and while his behavior toward his own family was erratic at times, a constant theme throughout his life can be found in his large family, or the almost tribal aspects of the group of people he collected around him. Open planning, or the combination of different interior spaces and ennobling certain activities of the family, the rituals of the fireplace and dining, is a common feature of all Prairie School dwellings. While the form of the buildings: the flat roofs, the geometrical trim, the spaces, may be different for their time, the social program of the houses is conservative. As Wright wrote in an essay of 1908, "radical though it be, the work is dedicated to the cause conservative in the best sense of the word."[19]

An explanation of the appeal of the Prairie School to Iowans in the years 1900–1930 has to take into account this statement of Wright's. In spite of the attempt by some of the architects and later historians to associate the Prairie School with a liberal and progressive ideology, this was not the interpretation of the clients of the period.[20] Certainly a politically liberal architectural style would not generally appeal to the Republican, rural people of Iowa.[21] In actuality the Prairie School had little if any ideological content on either side of the political spectrum. Between Prairie School clients in Iowa and other states, certain similarities exist. The vast majority of Prairie School buildings were built in three areas: cities, suburbs, and resorts. In Iowa all the Prairie School buildings were located in towns or cities. None is on farms or the open prairie. The word "Prairie" was a symbolic regional association and not a statement of location or usage.

Occupationally, the Iowa clients who can be identified are businessmen or professional men from the upper middle class of their towns. In status and occupation they are similar to many of Wright's clients. The prosperity of the "Golden Age of Agriculture," 1897–1920, spilled over into the towns and cities of Iowa, at the same time as the farm population was declining and the more urban areas experienced growth. Banks profited most from this prosperity and shift, and it is significant that three of the more important Prairie School building campaigns in Iowa were related to banking interests: Mason City, Cedar Rapids, and Grinnell. The acceptance of the Prairie School by the substantial businessmen who needed the image of respectability, indicates its nonradical nature.

In Sinclair Lewis's *Mainstreet* Gopher Prairie is the generally perceived image of cultural life in the farming Midwest during the years 1900–1930. Yet as Carol Kennicott constantly discovered, the town denizens had an awareness of the outside world and accepted new ideas as long as they were not too radical or outlandish. Certainly an oversimplification, *Mainstreet* (1920) does give an insight into midwestern life of the period. Why did rural midwesterners commission Prairie Style buildings? There are several answers. The style was seen as a regional expression as the architects frequently proclaimed. In a more positive manner than other architecture of the period, the Prairie house asserted the traditional elements of status, shelter, security against the outside world, and family solidarity in the face of disintegrating institutions. There is the possibility that the clients did not know what they were getting. The Prairie School building was simply a choice among many competing styles: Tudor, Swiss, Bungalow, Colonial Revival, and Italian, shown side-by-side in the *Ladies' Home Journal* or plan books. It was more visually appealing than other popular styles. Iowa's orientation, culturally as well as economically, was to Chicago rather than any other midwestern metropolis. Ideas, styles, and fads began in Chicago. Certainly the relative popularity of the Prairie School there stimulated Iowans to commission Prairie School buildings. The Prairie School in Iowa involves a number of complicated cultural issues, but its success was related to the emulation of more metropolitan centers. Ultimately, this was the reason for its eventual decline and failure in the later 1920s.

THE PRAIRIE SCHOOL IN MASON CITY

Mason City is unique not only in Iowa but in the United States, for two reasons: first, for the high quality of its Prairie School architecture, and second, for the only extensive example of Prairie School planning anywere. The story is complex since it stretches over ten years and included a great number of Prairie School architects.[22]

In 1908 Frank Lloyd Wright was offered his first Iowa commission by two Mason City lawyers and businessmen, J. E. E. Markeley and James E. Blythe. The project included a new bank, offices, and a connecting hotel.[23] During this period Mason City was undergoing dramatic growth and political and economic rivalries sprang up such as the one between Markeley's and Blythe's City National Bank and the McNider family's First National Bank. This led to two new bank buildings on opposite corners of the same street within a year. Frank Lloyd Wright entered the picture through Markeley whose daughters attended the Hillside School in Spring Green, Wisconsin, owned by aunts of Wright's. In 1902 when Markeley's eldest daughter entered, Wright had just completed his second building for the school, a native limestone and oak structure. Markeley and Wright became friends and in 1908 Wright received the bank and hotel commission (Cat. 28).

Wright's designs for the City National Bank and Hotel are vintage Prairie School. Built out of a buff colored glazed brick with wide projecting eaves the buildings stretch along the south side of the city square. The design for the bank is related to two earlier projects, "A Village Bank" published in the *Brickbuilder,* and a bank for Dwight, Illinois, both of which were solid cubical blocks pierced by rectilinear openings (Fig. 7). In the City National Bank, blank lower walls and the tall entrance encase the banking activities and provide a monumental air. Lighting is provided by clerestory windows; office space is located on the upper floor. Florid ceramic tile ornament and leaded glass is used at the openings in contrast to the solid planar walls. The hotel is simply two three-story pavilions linked by a low central pavilion that contains the lobby and cafe.

During this period, Wright also obtained two other commissions in Mason City. The first, a small house for Dr. George C. Stockman, a friend of Markeley's, was based on Wright's "A Fireproof House for $5,000," except that it was constructed of wood and stucco instead of concrete (Cat. 43). The other was a residence for Joshua Melson, a

Fig. 7. "A Village Bank,"
Frank Lloyd Wright, 1901,
William Drummond, delineator
(Brickbuilder, *August, 1901).*

business associate of Markeley's and Blythe's, who owned a tract of land along Willow Creek. This area known as Rock Crest/Rock Glen was a semiwild tract bordered on one side by steep limestone cliffs, a former quarry site, and on the other by a gently sloped glen. It had been bypassed as unbuildable when Mason City had developed eastward and hence was a significant open space of 18 acres only three blocks from downtown. Markeley, who lived adjacent to the Rock Glen area, introduced Wright to Melson who broached an idea of developing the site as a restricted residential area and commissioned Wright to design a house for him (Fig. 8). Wright's design was never built but in view of the later house Melson commissioned and built, it is of interest. Essentially, Wright's design is for a house on a

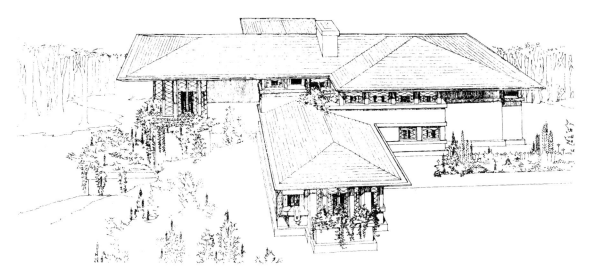

Fig. 8. Mason City, Iowa. Joshua Melson house, project, Frank Lloyd
Wright, 1908, Marion Mahony, delineator (Ausgeführte Bauten).

11

level site and is well set back from the cliffs. To what extent Wright considered the remainder of Melson's development is unknown, because at this juncture certain events occurred that foreclosed any future work for Wright in Mason City.

In late 1909, Wright, this immensely successful architect, abandoned his wife and six children and departed for Europe with another woman, the wife of a former client. The uproar was tremendous. America was still prudishly conservative and newspapers picked up the story. In Mason City it received four headlines. Wright turned his office work over to various assistants, and although he returned to the Midwest in late 1910, both his clientele and the nature of his work were significantly different. With this, Wright in a sense retreated within himself and his life for the next twenty years was a complicated mixture of tragedy and absurdity. For many years his clients were largely outside the Midwest: in California and Japan. But by 1909 he had given a major impetus to the developing Prairie School. Later in life Wright would look back bitterly at those he felt were copying him, but in 1908 while speaking of his work he said that ''for me the one real proof of the virtue inherent in this work will lie in the fact that some of the young men and women who have given themselves up to me so faithfully these past years will some day contribute rounded individualities of their own, and forms of their own devising to the new school.''[24] The broad outlines of the Prairie School had been laid down, now it was time for other individuals to give it a new sense of form and direction.

The City National Bank and Park Inn were completed in August and September 1910, respectively, under the direction of William Drummond (1876–1946). Drummond was a talented young architect who had worked briefly for Sullivan and then for Wright in the years 1899–1901 and 1903–1909.[25] He had left Wright over nonpayment of salary, a frequent occurrence in Wright's studio. A small Prairie School house for Curtis Yelland located on a lot bought from Melson across the street from the Rock Crest tract appears to have been designed by Drummond during this period (Cat. 44). Squat and severely rectilinear in shape, the Yelland house has Drummond's trademarks of double batten siding and emphatically stated trim. The Yelland house is derived from Wright's $5,000 house scheme and has an L-shaped living and dining area. Handsome wood trim, built-in cabinets, buffet, and sofa stress the continuity of the spaces. A unique feature is a mezzanine sitting room located on the stairlanding between the first and second floors.

Joshua Melson still had ideas about the Rock Glen development and after waiting a short time he approached a former member of Wright's office, Marion Mahony. Significantly, Wright was back in the Chicago area, but Melson evidently never approached him again. Marion Mahony (1871–1962) was the second woman to graduate from the Massachusetts Institute of Technology School of Architecture (1894) and the first woman licensed as an architect in the state of Illinois. She had worked for Wright at irregular intervals between the years 1895–1909, and was highly valued by him as a designer and renderer.[26] It is through her talent that we see much of Wright's work from these years, for she prepared the remarkable pen and ink drawings with their flat Japanese character that Wright published as his work (Figs. 2, 5, 8). On Wright's departure for Europe in 1909, a

12

portion of his work had been turned over to Hermann von Holst who subsequently engaged Marion Mahony to oversee it. At the time Melson approached Mahony, she had just been married to Walter Burley Griffin (1876–1937), who had also been in Wright's studio, but left in 1906 for the usual reason, nonpayment of salary. Griffin had attended the University of Illinois where he had studied architecture, landscape architecture, and urban planning, graduating in 1899.[27] At first Mahony tried to beg off from Melson with the excuse of too much work, but then as she relates: "The spark caught and I said I thought I could do that [make a perspective drawing of the area] but if it was a landscape scheme he ought to talk with Mr. Griffin about it, and I showed him some of Griffin's houses, etc. He had a talk," Mahony relates and "had Griffin go down to Mason City for a day at the end of which the two gentlemen signed away their so-called liberties in a contract which bound each of them to do nothing on the property without Mr. Griffin's approval."[28]

The agreement Mahony refers to actually was signed by four men, Joshua Melson, J. E. E. Markeley, James E. Blythe, and William J. Holahan. They agreed to preserve the natural beauty of the Rock Glen area, to clear out debris that had collected (for some years it had been used as a garbage pit) and use the land only for residential purposes. Griffin's plan called for the placement of houses around the perimeter of the site, both on the cliffs or crest and in the glen, creating a wall between the street and the open space that served as a common private park (Fig. 9). Nature was not to be left raw, extensive grading and filling was completed, plans were made (though never carried out) for a dam and bridge and for extensive landscaping in both local and imported plants. The designs Griffin submitted were varied though all were in the Prairie School idiom. Linking the houses thematically is rough-faced limestone ashlar from the former quarry that is used as a base and terraces for all the houses except one, the Rule house. The native limestone is used also for a low wall and gate posts for the houses along State, Rock Glen, and First streets. Typically the houses

Fig. 9. Mason City, Iowa. Rock Crest-Rock Glen development project, Walter Burley Griffin, 1912, Marion Mahony, delineator (Burnham Architectural Library).

13

are designed with service facilities and communication spaces clustered together toward the street leaving unobstructed living spaces with vistas oriented towards the park. However, the houses are separate from nature, and rarely is access given directly on the ground, but rather through halls, verandas, or terraces. Of the sixteen or so houses Griffin projected for the scheme, only five of Griffin's designs ever were built.

Chronologically, the first was the Harry D. Page house, 1912, on the north side of the development on land purchased from Blythe (Cat. 38). Page had been so interested in the concept of the development that he had earlier requested plans from Purcell and Elmslie, a Minneapolis firm working in the Prairie School idiom. Griffin's design for Page was a rather high tight house with projecting gables flaring at the eaves. It was built with a reinforced concrete frame that is directly expressed on the exterior.

The second house to be completed was commissioned by Blythe in 1912, but sold shortly after completion to Arthur Rule, his law partner (Cat. 40). The source for the Rule house is Wright's "fireproof house" (Fig. 5), but reworked into an entirely new design. Square and symmetrical, Griffin emphasizes the corner stucco piers, making the house more of a harboring image. The interior of the Rule house is particularly fine, built into the corner piers are cabinets and book cases; gumwood is used extensively for the trim, including the exposed ceiling beams.

Solidness and density are Griffin's personal trademarks, and he carried this further in what is undoubtedly the prize of the Rock Glen development, Joshua Melson's own house (Cat. 36). Instead of placing the house well back from the cliffs as Wright had done, Griffin dropped the house over the cliffs, giving in Mahony's words, "finish to the quarry face and commanding views up and down the river." A primitive image, the house is constructed out of the limestone of the cliffs and appears to grow or be hollowed from the precipice. Great concrete mullions and voussoirs articulate the openings in this nearly solid hunk of rock.

The fourth house was for James Blythe. It was designed in 1913 and built entirely of reinforced concrete: walls, floors, and roof (Cat. 27). Again the house is symmetrical, its extending subsidiary wings recalling the sixteenth-century Italian villas designed by Andrea Palladio, as does also its removal from the ground by a terrace. Between Griffin's initial plans and the completed house certain changes were introduced, the veranda and balcony were enclosed for year-round use, and the garage was enclosed at one end, but given a picture window to balance with the other wing. On the interior space, defining wood trim is integrated with cove lighting. The fireplace is covered in Italian tile in a geometric pattern designed by Marion Mahony. Built-in cabinets have leaded glass doors that continue the pattern of the exterior windows.

Of Griffin's other designs for the development, one for William J. Holohan, who owned an interest in Melson's property, was never built (Fig. 10). Designed for a sloping site, the elemental piers for the veranda and lower floor give it a tree house quality. Marion Mahony Griffin's contribution to all these buildings is uncertain; certainly she advised and she did produce the wonderful renderings.

14

*Fig. 10. Mason City, Iowa. William J. Holohan house project, Walter Burley Griffin, 1912 or 1913 (*Western Architect, *August, 1913).*

In May, 1912, just before work was getting underway on the Rock Crest-Rock Glen development, it was announced that Griffin had won the competition for the new capital of Australia at Canberra. He was to become the official architect and consequently he spent considerable time out of the United States in the next two years, until 1914 when he and Marion moved there permanently. The game of musical chairs continued at Mason City, for Griffin turned over his practice and the supervision of unfinished buildings to Barry Byrne (1883–1967) in late 1913. Byrne had received his architectural training in Wright's studio between the years 1902 and 1908. Then after a short illness he moved west to Seattle and then to Southern California.[29] For the Rock Glen development Byrne oversaw the completion of the Sam Schnider house that Griffin had designed in 1913 (Cat. 41). Byrne introduced a few changes in the fenestration, but essentially the design was Griffin's with a spectacular story-and-a-half living room and the dining room opening from a half level higher from the rear. Full of spatial variety, the Schnider residence indicates Griffin's further release from Wright's influence with his own interest in a vertical movement of space.

Byrne went on to produce several more designs for the masters of the Rock Crest-Rock Glen enclave. Joshua Melson's wife died in 1915 and Byrne designed for him a simple yet moving mausoleum constructed of rough faced ashlar (Cat. 37). For James Blythe, Byrne also designed a house for his daughter and son-in-law, Hugh Gilmore, a rather austere boxy dwelling of stucco perched on a rough ashlar base (Cat. 33).

Byrne's last-built design for the Rock Glen enclave was the Edward V. Franke house adjacent to the Gilmore house. This house again combined the same elements but was not nearly so distinctive (Cat. 32).

Byrne also drew up plans for several other houses but none came to fruition. An argument with a client, Samuel Davis Drake, caused Byrne to be fired and Drake's house was subsequently erected after designs by a young Mason City architect and builder, Einar Broaten (Cat. 30). The house may well owe something to Byrne's original plans, though stylistically it is more akin to the Rule house, Walter Burley Griffin's work. Square in plan with a projecting solarium and an attached garage, the Drake house is awkwardly composed, with the symmetrically identical windows placed on the garden side. Sited on the middle of the lot, the opportunity for outdoor views, such as Griffin had taken advantage of, was compromised.

By 1917 the work of the major Prairie School architects was completed in Mason City; out of the projected sixteen houses, only eight had been built. However, in the neighborhood of Rock Crest-Rock Glen a number of other houses were erected in a proto-Prairie School style with wide overhanging eaves, simple geometrical shapes, and involved ornament (Cat. 31, 39). About the designers of these, little is known; they were local architects and builders, or possibly the elusive Einar Broaten. Broaten produced a number of designs in Mason City and the area, and his signature can be seen in the treatment of a gable roof, or an entrance motif. One of Broaten's most unusual designs is the Critelli house in Mason City, a charming yet naive attempt to produce Griffin's magnificent Melson house (Cat. 29). Broaten's work and that of his local contemporaries can be seen as a dissolution of the Prairie Style of the Chicago based architects to a local and vernacular level.

In the 1950s, Curtis Besinger, a recent product of Wright's Taliesin fellowship, was asked to design a house for Tom McNider to fit on a site between the Rule and Page houses (Cat. 34). The McNider house thus continues the unbroken line of seven Prairie School houses down State Street and around Rock Glen Drive, one of the largest ensembles in the United States, and the only true example of Prairie School planning.

LOUIS SULLIVAN IN IOWA

Louis Sullivan's career after 1900 and until his death in 1924 was largely confined to the design of small banks and stores in midwestern farming towns. A comedown for a man who had been at the top of his profession, these small buildings are important for several reasons. First, they are splendid visual examples of his attempt to renew American architecture which became inspirations to his midwestern followers. Second, Sullivan's intensive development of their forms, and the passion and emotion he poured into them, lifts them from the level of a banal box on Main Street into ennobling gestures of the life of the town.

Sullivan's career as the designer of small-town banks began in 1906 when he designed a new building for the National Farmer's Bank of Owatonna, Minnesota (Fig. 11). Simple forms and complex details are the main themes. Composed as a nearly square main block punctured by high-arched windows, the exterior is a monumental envelope for a rich interior. Clearly, the building somewhat resembles Wright's earlier village bank project (Fig. 7), and one can see Sullivan taking inspiration from his former student.[30]

Probably the commission for the People's Savings Bank in Cedar Rapids, Iowa, 1909–1911, resulted from the publicity the Owatonna bank had received (Cat. 3). For the Cedar Rapids bank Sullivan abandoned the previous solution of square volume and restudied the bank's program. Here the requirements were for more subsidiary office space,

Fig. 11.   Owatonna, Minnesota. National Farmers' Bank, Louis Sullivan, 1906–1908.

and these resulted in an entirely different form. Sullivan designed a building with a central banking room, about 25 by 50 feet, surrounded by subordinate offices and spaces. Montgomery Schuyler, a contemporary critic, described the People's Savings Bank: "The building is thus clearly designed from within outward. The exterior is the envelope of the interior reduced to its very simplest expression."[31] Sullivan's famous dictum, "form follows function," is revealed in the high central block of the lobby surrounded by the low mass of the offices. Ten steel columns covered with wood carry the clerestory walls which provide a superb setting for a series of murals by Chicago artist Allen Philbrick depicting the agricultural life of Iowa. Low partitions separate the public space from the tellers and the offices. Only the consulting room, the coupon room, and the waiting rooms for men and women are enclosed. Such designated waiting rooms were typical features of farming community banks of this period. They were intended as resting stations for the rural customers on their daylong trips into town. As Schuyler wrote: "whoever enters the bank can see through it from end to end and from side to side." It is, he continued, "the habitation of a highly organized and highly specialized machine, in which not only provision is made for every function, but expression given to every provision."[32] On the exterior, red tapestry brick, small swaths of red terra-cotta mouldings, and Sullivan's viney ornament give a simple and austere appearance.

The construction of the People's Savings Bank was directed by its Vice-President, Fred Shaver, a member of an old Cedar Rapids family. Shaver, impressed by the principles of the Prairie School elucidated by Sullivan, had his home remodeled in the Prairie School style (Cat. 5). The house was originally built in 1909 for Frank W. Gates by a Clinton, Iowa, architect. In the next year Shaver purchased it and the remodeling was carried out. Stylistically the house is in the Prairie School idiom with its severe rectilinear form, overhanging eaves, open interior plan, and casement windows. Local tradition associates Sullivan with the house, but no evidence exists, and the ornament and the leaded glass windows are unlike Sullivan's motifs. Possibly the remodeling was by a local architect directed by Ossian C. Simmonds (1855–1931) of Chicago, the landscape architect who was hired by Shaver to lay out the grounds. Little of Simmonds' landscaping remains, but his style, utilizing native midwestern plant materials, is akin to the Prairie School architecture.[33] A small fire station in Cedar Rapids, designed by local architect Robert R. Mayberry in the Prairie School style, may provide a clue to the author of the Shaver remodeling (Cat. 6).[34]

Also in Cedar Rapids is another Sullivan building, Saint Paul's Methodist Episcopal Church, with a complicated history (Cat. 4). In early 1910, Purcell, Feick, and Elmslie, the Minneapolis firm of architects, were asked by T. H. Simmons, the head of the church board, to submit plans for a new building. Both William Gray Purcell (1880–1965) and George Grant Elmslie (1871–1952) had been in Sullivan's office (Purcell for a short period in 1903), while Elmslie had assumed after the departure of Wright the position as chief draftsman and designer and had stayed on until late 1909 taking a major part in the design of Iowa buildings such as the Owatonna and Cedar Rapids banks.[35] The third partner,

18

George Feick, Jr., was trained as an engineer, but contributed little to the firm's work and withdrew completely in 1913. Purcell had gone to Cedar Rapids to talk to the church board and had submitted plans for a cruciform church with a separate bell tower[36] (Fig. 12). At this point Sullivan entered the scene, either through Purcell's mention of his role as the fountainhead of an American architectural style, or as a result of the new bank then under construction. In any event, Purcell and Elmslie were displaced by Sullivan. His project of late 1910 was for a large rectangular building housing the Sunday School and social ac-

Fig. 12.   Cedar Rapids, Iowa. Saint Paul's Methodist Episcopal Church project, W. G. Purcell and G. G. Elmslie, 1910 (Northwest Architectural Archives, University of Minnesota).

19

tivities with an attached semicircular auditorium and projecting stair towers for the entrances. Rising from the center of the mass was a richly ornamented bell tower. Ample communication existed between the two main functional areas and the board was pleased by the design. But problems existed about the cost, and after one redesign, Sullivan resigned in a huff in March, 1912. However, the board kept his plans and turned them over to an obscure Chicago architect, W. C. Jones, instructing him to cut costs and get the design within the $100,000 budget. Jones manhandled the design, and just prior to ground-breaking in March, 1913, Elmslie was called back in to correct the worst injustices.[37] Completed in May, 1914, the church retains Sullivan's essential concept except for minor modifications and the complete elimination of his ornament or the substitution of catalogue stock for it. A totally new design for the Methodist church had been attempted, one that did not copy inappropriate forms from other faiths, but rather was designed around the concept of a spoken and visual nonprocessional service, with emphasis on the teaching and social aspects of parish life.

Sullivan's three other Iowa buildings are essentially solid cubical masses that contain interior volumes of space. In Clinton he designed a four-story department store of the John D. Van Allen and Son Company (Cat. 12). Horizontal bands of windows wrap around two sides of the building and the ground floor is completely open for display. Constructed of a steel frame and covered with long Roman bricks purple in color, black marble is used as a frame at the base and dabs of blue, green, gray, and white terra-cotta tiles are worked in as ornamental motifs. Thin mullions run vertically up the front, completely separate from the structure, and break into foliations. For Henry C. Adams in Algona, Sullivan produced a simple and unassuming box, direct in its statement as a proposed bank (Cat. 1). Unfortunately, Adams never received his bank charter and the building has been used for a variety of purposes over the years. The box shape has been carefully studied, the entrance is arranged inside a deep recess of projecting piers carrying planters, while the side wall contains nine deep-set windows. Subtle variations in brick pattern, small terra-cotta panels and mouldings, and the leaded glass are the only ornaments on the handsome shell. The Merchants National Bank at Grinnell continues the theme of the volumetric box and is perhaps Sullivan's finest late building (Cat. 18). It presents also one of the most interesting cases of Prairie School patronage, since one of its directors, Benjamin Ricker, also commissioned a house designed by Walter Burley Griffin.

In 1911, Griffin had been asked by a Grinnell businessman, Elbert W. Clark, Jr., for a design for a housing development (Fig. 13). Griffin laid out the subdivision following the contours of the land and spread the house sites to preserve open space and give each a view. Unfortunately, nothing ever came of this but two related commissions did result, the Clark Memorial Fountain (destroyed) and a house for Benjamin J. Ricker (Fig. 14 and Cat. 19). The fountain is an example of Griffin's adoption of Japanese motifs, indicative of his eclectic assimilation of such exotic themes as the pre-Columbian motifs in the Blythe house in Mason City (Cat. 27). The Ricker house is Griffin at his mature best, a solid rectangular

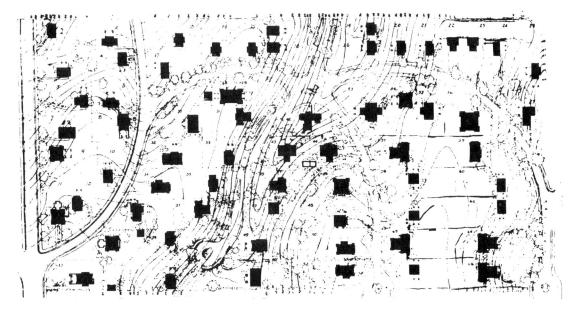

Fig. 13. Grinnell, Iowa. Clark resub-division project, Walter Burley Griffin, 1911 (Western Architect, *August, 1913).*

Fig. 14. Grinnell, Iowa. Clark Memorial Fountain, destroyed (date uncertain), Walter Burley Griffin, 1911 (Western Architect, *August, 1913).*

block covered by a long gabled roof and articulated by four massive corner piers that are intercut at the top by sleeping porches (Cat. 19). The long sides are further subdivided by eight bays and the entrance is placed asymmetrically in one of the center bays. Typical of Griffin's planning, the house is a self-enclosed entity with little direct contact with the out-of-doors; a cement porch with a low balustrade is used at the entrance and access to the garden is controlled through the attached veranda. Simple wooded trim and cove lighting is used on the ground floor, while on the second floor each of the bedrooms has an individual tent ceiling.

In autumn, 1913, the directors of the Merchants National Bank decided they needed a new building and Ricker took charge of procuring an architect.[38] By this time Griffin was heavily involved in his Australian work and while Barry Byrne was available and was to add a garage to Ricker's house, still Sullivan was selected. Most likely Ricker knew of Sullivan's work both through Griffin and also through the substantial publicity that had surrounded his other banks. According to local tradition, Sullivan arrived in Grinnell, met the building committee, purchased a pad of yellow paper and a ruler, and for three days sat in the old bank across the street from the new site sketching his proposal.[39]

The Merchants National Bank was one of Sullivan's strong boxes or "jewel boxes" as he called them (Cat. 18). Located on the corner of Fourth Avenue and Broad Street, the site was one of the most prominent in town—across from the Clark Memorial Fountain. The bank's position as the bedrock upon which the financial stability of the town and the surrounding farmland rested was explicitly stated. Essentially a two-story building, Sullivan lowered the street windows and emphasized the entrance and side windows, giving the building a monumental dignity far beyond its nominal size. On the exterior, wire-cut shale brick varying from a dark blue to a golden brown is offset by the gold leaf colonets of the side window, the leafy dark brown and gold terra-cotta cornice, and the extraordinary buff colored terra-cotta of the entrance. This motif, an excrescence supported by piers, is a series of squares, diamonds, circles, and foliated patterns that ripple outward, a keyhole that unlocks the strong box. Guarding either side of the entrance are two gilded gryphons. The interior is one of Sullivan's most successful, a simple two-story volume of space, calm in feeling, with the offices and tellers' cages projecting into it.[40] Swaths of color enliven the space, dark red brick is used for the partitions and lower portions of the wall, the upper section is white plaster; gilded terra-cotta is used for a band over the bank vault and the teller's cages; frosted glass and oak for the square electroliers; luminescent yellow, green, lavender, and peacock blue glass for a forty foot long side window; pink and cream for the skylight; and red, blue, green, and gold for the rose window. It is a brilliant sunset to a distinguished career.

PRAIRIE SCHOOL VARIATIONS

The Prairie School was created not by a single person nor confined to any narrow stylistic definition. From its early beginnings, it spread to a wide group of architects that remained consistent to certain basic principles and yet introduced personal variations.

22

BARRY BYRNE (1883-1967)

One example of individualization is the work of Barry Byrne in Fairfield and Keokuk. The Dr. James F. Clarke house, 1915, in Fairfield, is a forcefully composed mass of two interlocking rectangles, clean and precise, topped by two low pitched gables (Cat. 17). Semicircular windows soften the hard-edged geometry of the building and impart an ambiguous scale. On the interior, Byrne was assisted by Alfonso Iannelli who designed the furniture and rugs. A total design, it is one of Byrne's best works. An interesting clue to the client's reaction is that Mrs. Clarke originally wanted a Colonial design, but her husband prevailed.[41] Byrne's design for C. M. Rich, 1916, in Keokuk is not nearly as distinguished (Cat. 24). A large house with an uneasy massing, it is more eclectic in style, and its design draws from English Arts and Crafts and the California Spanish revival rather than from its own midwestern site.

GEORGE W. MAHER (1864-1926) AND ROBERT C. SPENSER, JR. (1865-1935)

The character of stylistic continuity can best be seen in two works in Waukon, Iowa, for the Hager family, by George W. Maher and Robert C. Spenser, Jr. Both Maher and Spenser knew Wright and Sullivan, but never worked for them and so developed independently. George Maher was an independently minded Chicago architect popular in the suburbs and involved with complicated design theories intended to create an expressive architecture.[42] Frequently the theories seem to overwhelm his design and he presents an uneven development. His J. H. Hager house in Waukon, 1907, is an example of his best work (Cat. 62). Solid and symmetrical with slightly off-balanced windows, it has the horizontals of the midwestern landscape combined with elements derived from the English Arts and Crafts and the Austrian Secessionist movements. Robert Spenser had been a member of the mealtime club, the "Eighteen" and an active participant in Chicago Arts and Crafts activities.[43] Instrumental in popularizing the Prairie School through picturing its architecture in the articles he wrote for *House Beautiful,* Spenser's personal preferences were more Anglican in inspiration. The house he designed for the second Hager brother in Waukon is not revivalistic as many of his designs tend to be, but a sensitive and honest use of brick in traditional forms (Cat. 63).

WILLIAM GRAY PURCELL (1880-1965), GEORGE FEICK (1881-1945), AND GEORGE ELMSLIE (1871-1952).

One of the major concerns of the Prairie School was a house for the middle class that would provide an alternative to the standard development home. To this end Wright had proposed in 1906 his "A Fireproof Home for $5,000" (Fig. 5). Purcell, Feick, and Elmslie of Minneapolis were intensely interested in alternatives to middle class housing as their

A. B. C. Dodd house in Charles City illustrates[44] (Cat. 8). Taking their clue from the vernacular builder, Purcell and Elmslie adapted a standard, rectangular, clapboarded house with a gable roof and emphasized the planiarity and prismatic character by special trim. On the interior the living and dining rooms became nearly one space, opened to the exterior by a long picture window. Simple oak trim defines the flat wall planes. Interested in economy, the more Purcell and Elmslie cut their budget to compete with builder designed dwellings, the more they were forced away from custom designs and toward standard box types.

WILLIAM LA BARTHE STEELE (1875-1949)

William La Barthe Steele of Sioux City, Iowa, provides the most interesting case of individualization of the Prairie Style after 1915, both in Iowa and the Midwest as a whole. Born in Springfield, Illinois, Steele was trained as an architect at the University of Illinois, graduating in 1896 and then spending the next three years in Sullivan's office. After a few years with various architects in Pittsburgh, he was offered a position in Sioux City in association with an architect. In 1906 Steele opened his own office in Sioux City and quickly became the city's most prominent architect.[45] While his early work varies in quality and frequently exhibits medieval eclecticisms, Sullivan's influence on Steele can be seen in a number of commercial buildings that straightforwardly display their frame and are rectilinear in nature.[46] Sioux City was conservative aesthetically, and Steele could not find clients for the different looking designs of the Prairie School. His moment came though in 1915 when he was selected by limited competition as the architect of Sioux City's new Woodbury County Courthouse (Cat. 61). Unsure of his winning Gothic Revival scheme, Steele was able to convince the County Board of Supervisors that they deserved something better, a style of the Midwest. Eventually receiving permission, Steele invited his old friends, George Elmslie and William Gray Purcell, to come in as associate architects. Elmslie came to Sioux City from Minneapolis to take charge of the design. The concept presented in March, 1915, aroused protests as being too radical. However, after minor changes the supervisors approved the design in December, 1915; construction began in 1916; and the building was completed in March, 1918.

Steele was the executive in charge and contributed some features, but the design was largely Elmslie's with Purcell overseeing the sculpture of Alfonso Iannelli for the entrances and the murals of John Norton for the lobby.[47] Designed around a large lobby covered by a dome with the traditional civic symbol of a tower arising overhead, the building was split into two functional parts: the square base containing the major public facilities, courts, tax offices, and supervisor's meeting room; while offices, the law library, and an art gallery occupied the tower. The entire building, interior and exterior, is covered with a warm tan Roman brick (with raked horizontal joints) and then overlaid with an efflorescence of glazed terra-cotta ornament, white on the interior and polychrome on the exterior. Overall

24

the building gives the impression of an articulated frame. The entrance façade, with pronounced vertical piers, recessed spandrels, and a heavy cornice has an awkward air, not fully resolved. The side street and alley façades are more successful. They are composed of more substantial blank walls, intercut with superb leaded glass windows (small for offices and large for courtrooms), protected by thin cantilevered slabs. The rear side, the jail entrance, is also of interest with its functional disposition of parts and integrated fire escapes. Most exciting though is the tower with its multiplanes and dramatic triangular prow topped by an eagle designed by Iannelli. Unhappily, Iannelli's major sculpture over the two entrances is not so well integrated.

The lobby with its articulated piers, balconies jutting forward, colorful murals, great swaths of terra-cotta, and a large, leaded-glass dome simply overwhelms the viewer, and is one of the most exciting spaces in not only Iowa but the United States. Perhaps the glass dome, not visible on the exterior, is unsettling. It projects into the bottom story of the tower which is given over completely to windows for lighting. Next to the pyrotechnics of the lobby, the courtrooms are quiet spaces and yet they are the best features of the design. Elegant leaded-glass windows along the sides; tent-shaped skylights; brick lower walls topped by plain plaster; simple wooden and black marble trim; brick judges' benches; and custom designed electroliers give the courtrooms a rarely achieved humane quality. In sum, the Woodbury County Courthouse is a remarkable building, the only major public building in the Prairie Style. At the same time certain problems with enlarging the Prairie Style to a monumental scale can be noted; it was a style that succeeded best in a smaller, more domestic scale.

Having broken the ice with the "radical" courthouse, Steele found Sioux City citizens more accepting of Prairie School work in the next few years. His First Congregational Church, 1918, is a pastiche; the solid rectilinear quality of the walls mitigated by the inappropriate round-headed windows and the awkward dome (Cat. 52). Perhaps the church dome gives a clue to the origins of the dome in the courthouse. On the interior lush Sullivan ornament covers the ceiling.

Far more successful is his Knights of Columbus Hall, a handsome brick box with crisply handled projections. Devoid of ornament, its entire effect comes from the careful arrangement of punctures into the solid mass (Cat. 54). Similar in massing is Steele's Livestock National Bank, its surface enlivened by particularly fine Sullivanian ornament that surrounds bulls heads (Cat. 55).

Of the numerous homes Steele designed in the Prairie Style, the H. H. Everist residence, 1916–1917, is the most noteworthy (Cat. 53). Long horizontal volumes of space are stacked together, and tied to the site by outstretching terraces and pergolas. Forms basically Wrightian in origin are articulated by Sullivan-derived ornament. Stretching the entire length of the ground floor is a 90-foot long sweep of unobstructed space, encompassing porches and living and dining rooms.

Steele's influence can be seen in a 1927 house design by one of his former assistants for Frank Albertson (Cat. 51). A T-shaped plan and horizontal massing similar to the Everist house, along with Steele's trademark of a green-tile roof has frequently led observers to attribute the house to him rather than to its true architect, K. E. Westerlind. Steele continued his usage of the Prairie School idiom into the late 1920s in his two branch public libraries of 1924–1927 (Cats. 57–58). Treated simply with high brick walls, narrow stucco banding, prominent entrance piers, and overhanging eaves, they are some of Steele's most pleasing designs. A third branch library he designed in 1928–1929, the North Side Building, is in the neo-Tudor style, indicating the waning of the Prairie School influence. His Williges (women's store) of 1930–1931 incorporates on its street front, white glazed terra-cotta with Sullivanian motifs (Cat. 60). It is one of the last manifestations of the early Prairie Style in the United States.

LOCAL ARCHITECTS

Scattered across the state are many more examples of the Prairie School style by Chicago architects as well as local builders and designers (Cats. 21, 22). By 1910 the Prairie School style was no longer confined to the group of architects clustered around Wright and Sullivan, but it was being picked up by local builders and architects through the vehicle of magazines.[48]

The work of Einar Broaten in the Mason City area is merely one example of local manifestations of the style. Mortimore Cleveland, a Waterloo architect, produced numerous variations as in houses in Grinnell and Charles City (Cats. 7, 9, 20). In these cases there is a mixing of the Prairie School with the Craftsman aesthetic; his work has similarities to both. An example of a Craftsman home with Prairie School characteristics is the Gideon D. Ellyson residence in Des Moines where the plain stucco walls, the scale, and the trim are very close to the Prairie School vocabulary (Cat. 14), and yet the plans were done by the Craftsman Bungalow Company of Seattle, Washington, and then detailed by a local Des Moines firm. Other examples of the Prairie School influence in Des Moines are the Harwood and Dewey houses, 1907 and 1916 (Cats. 13, 15). The emphatic symmetry and the solid rectangular massing of the houses are reminiscent of the early works of Wright and also indicative of the return to symmetry by most of the Prairie School architects in the 1910s.

While Prairie School work can be found into the 1920s, by 1930 its time seemed past. The major architects had vanished or were otherwise occupied: Sullivan was dead, Wright hounded by marital difficulties, Purcell retired by health problems, Elmslie drifting, Griffin and Mahony in Australia, and Byrne doing eclectic church designs. In Sioux City, Steele's Prairie School designs were no longer accepted. This disbanding of the Prairie School group was at least one reason for the demise of the style, but other factors were also in operation. Changes in taste were at least one factor. Colonial Revival and Tudor designs were the chic mode in the metropolitan centers. The search for an American expression had spent its power by the mid-1920s, and the periodicals that had promoted the Prairie School before 1920 had either moved their offices to the East Coast or turned their attention elsewhere.[49] The Prairie School as a movement was in demise, but its principle had an enduring relevance that became apparent in a stirring restatement of force and vigor in the thirties, forties, and fifties.

The Second

BY CONNECTING the Prairie School of midwestern architecture to Frank Lloyd Wright, we can carry it forward into the 1930s and beyond. The houses in Iowa that Wright designed in the forties and fifties and those designed by men who worked for him in that period are examples of the extended category of the Prairie Style house. But Wright's personal taste alone does not account for a Prairie Style of building at midcentury. The principles of design that related composition of building parts to a geographical region in 1910 remained vital forty years later. A new way of applying these principles resulted from changes in American domestic life patterns in that period. As long as the Prairie Style of architecture is recognized by the expression of certain principles of spatial, material, and landscape continuity; of simplified massing and enriching detail; it extends beyond a strictly limited time period in Chicago at the beginning of the century. The presence of these principles relates later designs to the Prairie School. The continued use of those principles in new circumstances, a use which expresses the ideals even more clearly, surely deserves to be called an extension of the Prairie Style. This essay explains the Prairie Style as it was expressed regionally in the Midwest without attempting a complete assessment of the interaction of the changing forces in Wright's personal history, world economic conditions, or influences from the architecture of Europe or Japan.

TALIESIN

To begin this look at later Prairie Style work we must step back a moment before 1930. At the end of his Oak Park period, Wright developed a different domestic pattern for himself personally, and for his subsequent architectural expression when he built a house on family acreage west of Madison, Wisconsin, in 1911. The location of his studio-house-farm complex was remote. Placed in the midst of a beautiful rural landscape, Taliesin, as he called his country home, achieved a remarkable intimacy with land forms which even the large suburban lots around Chicago did not afford. Its one level expansiveness is free from strict axial planning as it wraps around a low hill. Domestic

Prairie School, 1930–Present

activities move easily past rugged limestone piers under wide eaves and out onto flagstone terraces. Much of the expansive informality of the Iowa houses he designed forty years later is derived from this beautiful home.

In 1936 Alfred Caldwell sensed the appropriateness of the forms and materials of the studio and house at Taliesin for a group of Park Shelters at Eagle Point Park on the Mississippi River north of Dubuque, Iowa. This Works Project Administration (WPA) project, completed in 1937, picks up almost intact the random limestone masonry walls, the wood-and-plaster-screen walls, and the horizontal window bands under the widely cantilevered hipped hoofs. The rustic materials are well used to shelter the informal functions of picnics and family outings (Cat. 16).

For fifteen years after finishing Taliesin Wright suffered personal tragedy, long absences from home while working in Japan, and severe legal and financial pressures. Not until 1928 could he return to a more or less settled life again at Taliesin. When Wright and his new bride Olgivanna created the Taliesin Fellowship in 1932 (an apprentice program for young architects) the economic situation in the country was bleak. He had few recent design commissions and the prospect indicated continued inactivity. The Fellowship, an extended "family" in the great house tradition of medieval times, pursued a way of life which included making buildings for the Fellowship, designing them for the occasional client, and practicing the spiritual exercises directed by Mrs. Wright. Thirty apprentices paid to become the first members of the Fellowship. Since 1932 many more came to be near Frank Lloyd Wright. Some stayed only for short periods; others who began in 1932 are still there. The first major project undertaken after making the neglected Taliesin and Hillside School facilities liveable was to build the immense model of Broadacre City: Wright's vision of the proper form for America and the ideal setting for his architecture. Later, apprentices also provided construction supervision for many of the houses in Iowa. This procedure clearly depended on a thorough assimilation of the master's ways which would permit the apprentice to function as his surrogate for on-the-spot decisions. As a result, the number of architects who went through this course of initiation and either matched the ineffable genius of Wright or maintained a personal integrity was small. The second generation of Prairie Style architects who came out of Taliesin are therefore not so varied or independently notable as those from the first generation.

THE USONIAN HOUSE

Within the stability of rural Wisconsin, surrounded by the masterful architectural creation of Taliesin, Wright turned his attention in 1935 to developing a simplified American house by reworking basic principles from his earlier work. He called the house type that evolved "Usonian," from the name he said Samuel Butler gave the United States. Wright saw the single family house in America as the crucial architectural problem growing out of the Depression. His solution is a direct descendant of the Prairie Style houses of the early years of the century. Differences that appear were made in response to new circumstances.

The seven houses Wright built in Iowa from 1945 to 1956 all possess features of the Usonian house type in its broadest definition. All but the Douglas Grant house in Cedar Rapids are on one floor. Floors are concrete carefully finished and given a dark red color. Heat is distributed by hot water tubes imbedded in the floor. Main living areas include dining tables and fireplaces. Glass doors allow living areas to open directly to ground level terraces. Cars are parked next to the house under cover, but not completely closed by walls. And a generally low, extended roofline settles easily over building and surrounding landscape.

An exterior feature of the typical Usonian house is a prefabricated, three-ply, board and batten wall that Wright introduced in 1936 for the Jacobs house near Madison, Wisconsin: the first Usonian dwelling. This solid wood wall appears in the Iowa houses only as interior partitions in the bedrooms that extend in a line from the main living space. The outside walls of the Iowa Usonians are all masonry, either brick or stone.

Precedents for some of the elements of planning and materials in the Usonian house can be discovered in the earlier Prairie Style houses. The principal living space which includes the dining area, either within the major volume or in an alcove, was a planning characteristic from very early in Wright's career. This combination provided the clearest expression of the principle of spatial continuity. Often, however, the more formal life style at the beginning of the century demanded some spatial segregation of distinct functions. Spur walls, screens, or ceiling patterns separated living from dining areas. Placing the dining table between the living room fireplace and the kitchen was an arrangement he had tried back in 1906 in the Glasner house north of Chicago. Even then this location was judged particularly appropriate for a home without domestic help. After the Depression such efficiency was even more appreciated.[1]

Another precedent for combining living and dining areas came from the Arts and Crafts movement in the late nineteenth century. William Morris, the leading English Arts and Crafts proponent, expressed the satisfactions available in a dwelling that did

30

not provide all the amenities of a properly urban life. His "sitting room where a healthy person does not cook much or sleep in generally, or engage in littermaking manual work," is a room where simplified forms of a whole day's activities could take place.[2]

In America an article in *House Beautiful* of 1905 described "A Bachelor's Cottage in the Country" whose large living, dining, study space produced a similar integration of functions.[3] Because the dwelling was for one person in an informal cottage out in the country, strict social patterns could be suspended. At the time Wright proposed similar arrangements in the 1930s, home design magazines of the time allowed such informal spatial arrangements only in vacation houses and weekend retreats whose remoteness and leisurely lifestyle did not demand proper domestic forms.[4]

The second distinctive element of Wright's Usonian house is the single level easily accessible to the ground. But this arrangement also was prefigured in his early work. Most of the early Prairie Style houses were two-story living units which makes Wright's one-story Cheney house of 1904 in Oak Park outstanding even among its contemporaries (Fig. 15). Its relation to the ground is an especially striking anticipation of later houses. From the living room, and connected to it by a row of glass doors, extends a ground level paved terrace. It is not a porch and it is not a narrow extension of the building foundation. The extent of the paving and its connection with the low walls that separate the lot from the sidewalk make the terrace as much a part of the ground as the

Fig. 15. Oak Park, Illinois. Edwin H. Cheney house, Frank Lloyd Wright, 1904, Marion Mahony, delineator (Ausgeführte Bauten).

31

house. A new, closer relation of living level to ground level is the most important characteristic of the Usonian house. Several circumstances allowed the formerly visual continuity, from inside to outside, to become a continuity on the level of human movement. The advances in glass technology provided larger plate glass sheets to open the living area onto the terrace. Hot water in the floor removed the barriers of radiators or hot air registers and an outdoor life pattern adopted from the Southwest and California gave a style to being in the open.

For all the conclusions drawn about prairie living, the early Prairie Style homes drew much of their sense of propriety from urban ideals. Suburbia was more open than the city, but propriety still required a certain elevation. The layers and padding that characterized formal clothing were carried over into the furred-out spaces that wrapped around proper living spaces. The early Prairie houses did away with a good deal of such space in attic and cellar; the Usonian house completed the task: little or no dead air space above heads, in walls, or underfoot. The same material was ideally continuous visually from outside to inside. That meant pulling the house right down on the ground. Since heat was introduced in the floor slab there was no need for air ducts threading their way behind interior surfaces and above ceilings.

The relationship to the land changed on a larger scale as well. The Depression was more visibly an urban phenomenon. Observers at the time noted how a new interest in having some ground of one's own appeared as a protection against the instability of urban economic interdependence. The automobile was the single most important piece of technology propelling the exodus from the city to one's acre of land. Wright had retreated to Taliesin, his Wisconsin home, during the Depression and kept occupied there building the model of a broad ideal of refuge and freedom. Broadacre City embodied important features the nation desired. Its astonishing congruence with the suburbs of the present proves how accurately it reflected deeply held values. Wright published the program of the new social and physical order of Broadacres in *The Disappearing City* (1932), *When Democracy Builds* (1945), and finally *The Living City* (1958). They each contain an explicit appreciation for the liberating joys of private land ownership. ''Spacious ground must be made available, on some fair basis. . . . City buildings in the new city will stand there free in its own greenery or lie long, flowing lazily and low on the prairie levels or stretching along the ridges above the ledges of the hills. At one with environment. Every man's home. . . . On his own sunlit sward or in wood or strand enhancing all other homes.''[5] The Anglicanisms in the last sentence uncover the historical ideal Wright had entertained for some time. In 1910 he had alluded to the rightness of cultural style, of building and land relationship that the English gentleman's life and house possessed.[6]

After the Depression Americans drove out to the peripheral farmland and put up houses. The Federal Housing Administration (FHA) provided critical financial structures and capital to build these dreams. Those visions were hardly baronial in extent though

32

often English in style. The white Georgian house with columns, bay windows, and fanlight was a common expression. Previous experimentation in housing styles had given way to an earnest search for security and stability which early American or European styles provided. What had been a native American architectural expression in the Midwest thirty years before was undone with surprising abandon. At the same time Wright was designing the Usonian home, using principles from his Oak Park, Illinois, days, houses in the Chicago area that had reflected those principles in 1915–1920 were being remodeled with white paint; the wide overhangs were being taken off and isolated windows were being distributed across the façade. Inside, wallpaper covered plaster, brick fireplaces were replaced by Georgian mantels and the straight, dark wood molding was removed or painted out.[7] Respectability reigned supreme. A more expansive country club style emerged as economic recovery proceeded. The seclusion that large lots provided was an important part of the opulent mode.

Wright saw his houses related to the land, not just from the inside, but from the outside as well. "Vision comes into grounds surrounding and he places appropriate gardens around him. Vistas of the landscape become part of his house and life just as his house becomes integral part of neighborhood landscape."[8] A congenial relation to the surrounding land was important not only through picture windows looking out, but was important to an observer looking at house and land from the outside. An unmistakable gap separated the idealistic cottager building his own house on his own land, from the financial resources needed to create this dream of carefully composed residential landscape.

The "radicalism" present in the Prairie Style, early or late, was a protest against stuffy conformity, but this fact did not prevent conspicuous consumers from seeking the notoriety of having a Frank Lloyd Wright house. Wright's firm belief in a natural aristocracy rising to the top through individual initiative and free expression predisposed him to value financial success not only for intellectual reasons, but for the freer hand it gave him to build lavishly. Both parties gained from the encounter. The home owner got something to flaunt to the world as another sign of success; Wright got a chance to try things in the house that someone with a personal sense of appropriateness may have rejected. Wright's own occasional lapses in taste may have been encouraged by an eager client willing to spend money.

The first house Wright designed in Iowa after the Depression was for Lowell Walter. It is located near the small town of Quasqueton, north of Cedar Rapids. In many ways it is a unique creation. Built by a road sufacing company owner as a kind of manor house in his hometown, it sits on a magnificent limestone bluff overlooking a bend in the Wapsipinicon River. A large gate and pylon inscribed with the family name announce its presence to the villagers. The style may diverge remarkably from the family headstone in the cemetery on the road to town, but the significance remains the same. Walter had contacted Wright about a house for this beautiful site in 1942. The plans for the house appeared in the *Ladies' Home Journal* in 1945.[9] It was not until materials became available after the war that construction began in 1948. Even then, the elaborate construction ran into considerable money. The elements of the house that are part of the Usonian type include the open living-dining room, the hall of bedrooms extending off one side, the concrete floor and the board and batten partitions in the bedroom wing (Cat. 49).

The simple Usonian ideal, however, had not been so lavishly treated before. To begin with the roof: instead of the three layers of 2×4s making up the roof, we have an immense 42-foot square concrete slab perforated by a raised central panel divided by skylights and by trellis-like openings beyond the windows. Along two of the 31-feet, 6-inch sides of the living room, called the Garden Room for its large central planting area, this visually light but structurally heavy slab is supported by twelve slender steel **T**'s. Between the steel are uninterrupted walls of glass. The view through them from the top of the hill is magnificent.

In the bedroom wing the beautiful board and batten partitions are assembled from plane and beveled walnut. This luxurious wood is carried throughout the structure, most surprisingly around the interior edges of the complex roof slab. Even the steel supports have strips of wood applied to them, successfully confusing their structural capabilities. The third major material in the house is a fine, hard, red brick whose precise character complements the exquisite carpentry.

Walter's house is one of the most complete designs Wright had the opportunity to create at this time. Wright was known to lament the effect produced on his houses when clients moved in; he could not say that about the Walters. From the dozen or so chairs of walnut, brass, and specially laminated foam rubber cushions, to the upholstery and draperies, to the colored glass fragments set in lighted recesses in the wall, Wright chose everything. The appointments found on shelves and tables were selected by Wright and John DeKoven Hill, one of his senior disciples from Taliesin, from the V. C. Morris Shop in San Francisco that Wright designed in 1948.

Two bathrooms are located in the bedroom wing projecting at a thirty degree angle from the garden room and entry. They are outfitted with a white, enameled metal unit combining toilet, lavatory, and tub/shower supplied by a central source of water. The Pullman-like compactness of this fixture, so much in sympathy with the efficient purpose of the Usonian house, is surprising in this "cost-is-no-object" country house. It is not used in any other house.[10]

Further evidence of the grandeur of this commission can be seen from the living room. Down the hill, perched on a huge boulder, is a riverside gazebo and boathouse. Its simplified function and smaller size make it a forceful combination of the elements found in the main house. Boats are drawn up from the water on rails by electric winches. Up the hill toward the trees is a "fire circle," an area enclosed by a low wall focusing on an outdoor hearth. The one gathering known to have made use of this ritual site is the visit of all the Taliesin apprentices with the Wrights after the house was finished in 1950. Wright referred to Lowell Walter as a "diamond in the rough," at least until Wright came along to give him a proper setting.[11]

Forty miles to the south of Quasqueton a young broadcaster in Cedar Rapids had acquired the end of a lovely promontory overlooking a creek. Douglas Grant and his wife had read about Wright and his ideas regarding domestic design and found much there they admired. They wrote to Wright at his Arizona home, Taliesin West, in 1945 and asked whether Wright would do a house for them. Wright did much for them by providing a house that met their stated needs wonderfully. They did much for themselves as they worked at every stage of construction. As a result, the Grants and their house are perfectly complementary; the efforts they have made living in the house, as well as constructing it, have been reciprocated by a house that created needs for a responsive environment because it satisfies them so completely (Cat. 2).

Their two-level house has the living-dining area and the kitchen on the low end of the hill and bedrooms at the entrance level on the high end of the slope. It is a variant on the original Usonian scheme. Beyond general location and time of construction, two other similarities link this house and the Walter's house: a concrete roof and its thin steel supports. The two-story living room, at the west end of the house, has glass on three sides. The roof is a 127-foot concrete slab supported at the glass end by a dozen steel **T**'s 20 feet high. From the entrance down a breathtaking staircase to the living room and the terraces beyond, the floors are stone slabs. Stone walls and chimneys were laid up in forms filled with thin slabs of limestone excavated from the property itself.

A satisfying sensation of shelter is felt around the towering fireplace mass as the living area moves back into the hill, up three broad steps to the dining area and under the first bedroom above. Because of the great openness and height at the end of the living room, this subtle closing of perspective is extremely effective.

A genuine simplicity and directness pervades this home, but it is not therefore a plain or uninteresting one. The long rectangle jutting out of the hillside is unmistakably dramatic. The hovering roof, starting low on the uphill side at the carport and sailing out toward the valley dispels any appearance of instability since it is so firmly anchored in the slope. In this house the limitations of budget prevented the edge of the roof from being covered by copper sheets embossed with a decorative pattern. The result seems more in keeping with the basic sensibility of the whole.

When Wright knew he was working with someone who would participate fully in the living experiences presented to them, he freely disclosed how much their lives would change in one of his houses. Oftentimes this involved sacrificing a bit of peripheral convenience for the integrity of the whole. The large glass doors in the Grant's living room had no provisions for screens. They inquired about this apparent oversight only to have Wright explain how they could spray or swat whatever flew in. The building process went in stages for nearly ten years, as house and family grew up together.

In the northern part of the state, Dr. Alvin Miller built a fine example of the Usonian house type, a small cottage-like dwelling along the Red Cedar River in Charles City. The L-shaped plan with the entry at the corner contains the combined living-dining area with fireplace and a wing toward the street with bath, bedroom, and carport. A single room projects toward the river and creates a partially enclosed terrace with the living room. The flat roof, concrete floors, and stone walls are all part of the Iowa Usonian type. The additional exterior materials of plaster and cypress bring out two other common materials in Wright's palette. The principle of continuity is again present in the materials that are the same inside and out, in the combination of living-dining areas, and in the terrace extending the living level beyond the glass wall of the living room (Cat. 10).

All the Iowa Usonian houses, including the Miller house, are laid out in plan with a regular geometrical unit repeated from one end of the house to the other and beyond into walls and terraces. This unit is most often a rectangle or square; the Miller, Grant, and Walter houses use a square grid to regulate the placement of walls and windows. Not every element falls exactly on the lines which are pressed into the concrete floors, but the lines set up a guide which ties all parts together.

In Oskaloosa Wright designed two houses within a year of each other. The first is the Jack Lamberson house, the only triangular or hexangular grid Wright used in Iowa. The second is the Carroll Alsop house of 1948. The Lamberson house is also the only one with a hipped roof, or rather a roof which turns all its sloped surfaces down to a horizontal eave as contrasted to the flat roofs of the first three houses or the gable in the Alsop house. The triangular pattern of the Lamberson house is most strikingly revealed in its roof as dramatic points extend beyond the red brick walls and over the slopes of its hilltop site. In spite of the departure from the typical Usonian model, this house does possess planning and materials that are associated with the other houses (Cat. 46, 47).

The Alsop house is a more elaborate form as to roofline. Its high gable creates a large volume in the living-dining area which is effectively modulated by the brick fireplace and chimney located at the highest part of the room. Here again we find dining table and chairs designed by the architect along with cabinets and shelving that are built into the structure. The range of bedrooms extending from the living area are partitioned by the board-and-batten wood system typical of the Usonian house, but here the scale of the wood strips and boards is enlarged giving a stately air to the hallway.

Both the Lamberson and Alsop houses contain kitchens without exterior exposure. The compensation for the lack of windows is made by skylights which create bright work spaces nonetheless. Since the kitchen is the major odor-causing area, its higher ceiling with ventilators at the top creates a natural air flow from the rest of the house through the kitchen and out the roof. It is probably the most problematical feature

36

when it is included in the plan, since work in the kitchen can be relieved by having something to look out upon.

At the very end of his career, Wright gave Iowa two lovely houses in the central part of the state: the Robert H. Sunday house in Marshalltown and the Paul Trier house in Johnston. The Sunday house is a crisp brick and stained wood structure which was initially proposed in a complicated cast block system Wright devised in the Richard Lloyd Jones house in 1929 in Arizona. Due to cost factors, the material was changed to brick for the Sundays. Its pavilion-like living room surrounded on two sides by tall brick piers is a bright and spacious room poised between the large windows and massive fireplace. Elements like the window-pier ensemble and the square plywood ceiling panels with recessed circular lights are variations on a house Wright designed for an exposition of his work in 1953 on the present site of the Guggenheim Museum in New York. This model house possessed a similarly grand living room where high windows on one side sought to balance the flood of light from the tall windows on the other (Cat. 23, 26).

A decorative element that both the Sunday and Trier houses share with the early Usonian houses is a perforated board and glass panel running along on top of walls, just below the ceiling. This intriguing light source is most often found in bedrooms and halls, but in the Trier house it takes the place of the large masonry piers of the Sunday house and provides a lovely vertical pattern dividing the glass doors leading from living area to terrace. The Trier house is another smaller-scale, less extravagant Usonian that surrounds one with warmth and a sense of well-being. It too is a wood and brick house with a high living room, but its dimensions are such that a comforting association with Wright's marvelously textured walls and window openings is never lost.

John Howe was one of the first apprentices who joined Wright at Taliesin in 1932. He remained with the Fellowship for several years after Wright's death in 1959. Subsequently, he set up his own architectural practice in Minneapolis. The Denniston house in Newton, Iowa, was designed by John Howe in 1961. The tradition of the Usonian house is continued here in all respects: living-dining areas open to exterior spaces; materials directly expressed. The large, beveled trellis that extends over the glass doors leading outside also projects inside to reinforce the continuity of movement and view through this side of the living room. Howe continued Wright's custom design practice in the dining room, built-in furniture, and in fabrics and lighting fixtures. At the entrance is a dynamic mural of wood and metal set on the masonry core containing fireplace and kitchen (Cat. 45).

And most fittingly, a second generation Wright follower, Curtis Besinger, added a Usonian dwelling in 1959 to the old Rock Glen development in Mason City for the son of one of the initial members of the Rock Crest group. The Tom McNider house is a hexagonal-grid house of wood and concrete block whose presence between two Griffin houses demonstrates how principles of domestic design for the Midwest can remain vital even as they are interpreted to fit successive cultural styles. Its low, geometric clarity, its simplicity of mass and complexity of detail are not superficially like its fifty-year-old neighbors for very many good reasons. But the ideal of a harmonious living pattern, both as an internal social, spatial, and material expression and as an external relation to the prairie remains a compelling force (Cat. 34).

In Sioux City, Besinger designed a less complete Prairie Style house in 1961. The William Nystrom house shows how easily Prairie Style details can be diffused into a more common domestic tradition (Cat. 55).

The validity of the cultural and material ideals of the Prairie Style has been demonstrated. At this time of reviewing our national roots, we in the Midwest can reexamine a domestic tradition completely our own which may well be the envy of the world.

Footnotes

INTRODUCTION

1. Nancy K. Morris Smith, ed., "Letters, 1903–1906, by Charles E. White, Jr., from the Studio of Frank Lloyd Wright," *Journal of Architectural Education,* 25 (Fall, 1971), 104.

SECTION 1

1. The undisputed authority is Carl Condit, *The Chicago School of Architecture* (Chicago and London: University of Chicago Press, 1964).
2. The basic study is Hugh Morrison, *Louis Sullivan, Prophet of Modern Architecture* (New York: W. W. Norton, 1935); also good is Albert Bush-Brown, *Louis Sullivan* (New York: Brazillier, 1960).
3. Louis Sullivan, *Kindergarten Chats and Other Writings,* ed. I. Athey, (New York: Wittenborn, 1947), p. 99. In addition to *Kindergarten Chats,* originally written 1901–1902, Sullivan wrote other essays and several books: *Democracy: A Man Search* (1908), *The Autobiography of an Idea* (1924), and *A System of Architectural Ornament According with a Philosophy of Man's Powers* (1924).
4. Wright has been the subject of numerous studies as well as his own proliferating pen; see his: *Autobiography* (New York: Longmans, Green, 1932), with several subsequent editions. The best studies are: Grant C. Manson, *Frank Lloyd Wright to 1910: The First Golden Age* (New York: Reinhold, 1958); Henry Russell-Hitchcock, *In the Nature of Materials: The Buildings of Frank Lloyd Wright, 1887–1941* (New York: Duell, Sloan and Pearce, 1942); and Robert C. Twombly, *Frank Lloyd Wright: An Interpretive Biography* (New York: Harper and Row, 1973).
5. The best work is H. Allen Brooks, *The Prairie School: Frank Lloyd Wright and His Midwest Contemporaries* (Toronto: University of Toronto Press, 1972); see also Mark L. Peisch,

The Chicago School of Architecture: Early Followers of Sullivan and Wright (New York: Random House, 1964).

6. See Robert C. Spencer, Jr., "Country Houses," *House Beautiful,* 19 (December, 1905), 23; and Wesley Shank, "The Residence in Des Moines," *Journal of the Society of Architectural Historians,* 29 (March, 1970), 56–59.

7. See Clay Lancaster, *The Japanese Influence in America* (New York: Walton H. Rawls, 1963).

8. Wesley Shank, "Hugh Garden in Iowa," *Prairie School Review,* 5 (Third Quarter, 1968), 43–47.

9. See Wright's Nathan G. Moore house, Oak Park, Illinois, 1895.

10. The relationship between the Prairie School and the earlier Chicago School is normally taken for granted, yet many differences are apparent that need further study.

11. Can be found in many places but see Louis Sullivan, "An Unaffected School of American Architecture: Will it Come?" *Artist,* 24 (January, 1899), xxxiii–iv; and Frank Lloyd Wright, "Prairie Architecture," *Modern Architecture* (1931), reprinted in *Frank Lloyd Wright: Writings and Buildings,* ed. E. Kaufmann and B. Raeburn (Cleveland and New York: World Publishing, 1960).

12. Vincent Scully, Jr., *The Shingle Style: Architectural Theory and Design from Richardson to the Origins of Wright* (New Haven: Yale University Press, 1955).

13. Brooks, *The Prairie School,* ch. 1; see also David A. Hanks, "Chicago and the Midwest," *The Arts and Crafts Movement in America 1876–1916,* ed. R. J. Clark (Princeton: Princeton University Press, 1972), pp. 57–78.

14. Frank Lloyd Wright, "The Art and Craft of the Machine," an address to the Chicago Arts and Crafts Society, Hull House, 6 March, 1901; reprinted in E. Kaufman and B. Raeburn, eds., *Frank Lloyd Wright: Writings and Buildings,* pp. 55–73.

15. John Crosby Freeman, *The Forgotten Rebel: Gustav Stickley and His Craftsman Mission Furniture* (Watkins Glen: Century House, 1966).

16. Henry H. Saylor, *Bungalows* (New York: McBride, Nast, 1911), p. 41.

17. Wright's designs in the *Ladies' Home Journal* appeared as: "A Home in a Prairie Town"; "A Small House with Lots of Room in It"; and "A Fireproof House for $5,000"; 18 (February, 1901), 17; 18 (July, 1901), 15; and 24 (April, 1907), 24. In *House Beautiful* they were, "Successful Homes III," 1 (15 February, 1897), 64–69; Alfred H. Granger, "An Architect's Studio," 7 (December, 1899), 36–45; and C. E. Percival, "A House on a Bluff," "Solving a Difficult Problem—Making the Most of a Narrow Lot," and "A House without a Servant," 20 (June, July, August, 1906), 11–13, 20–21, 13–14. Robert Spencer, a Chicago member of the Prairie School and designer of the O. J. Hager residence in Waukon, Iowa (Cat. 63), published a series of articles in *House Beautiful* between the years 1905–1909 with such titles as "Country House," "Plaster Houses and Their Construction," "The Abolition of the Backyard," and the like, that used Prairie School houses as illustrations.

18. Norris Kelly Smith, *Frank Lloyd Wright: A Study in Architectural Content* (Englewood Cliffs, N.J.: Prentice-Hall, 1966); Twombly, *Frank Lloyd Wright;* and his "Saving the Family: Middle Class Attraction to Wright's Prairie House, 1901–1909," *American Quarterly,* 27 (March, 1975), 57–72.

19. Frank Lloyd Wright, "In the Cause of Architecture," *Architectural Record,* 23 (March, 1908), 3.

20. The best consideration is Leonard K. Eaton, *Two Chicago Architects and Their Clients, Frank Lloyd Wright and Howard Van Doren Shaw* (Cambridge: M.I.T. Press, 1969); see also, Brooks, *The Prairie School,* p. 25.

21. Leland L. Sage, *A History of Iowa* (Ames: Iowa State University Press, 1974), ch. 13–15, and 18; see also Dorothy Schwieder, ed., *Patterns and Perspectives in Iowa History* (Ames: Iowa State University Press, 1973), especially Thomas T. McAvoy, "What Is the Midwestern Mind?" pp. 3–24.

22. Much of this section is based on Robert E. McCoy, "Rock Crest-Rock Glen: Prairie School Planning in Iowa," *Prairie School Review,* 5 (Third Quarter, 1968), 5–39.

23. Wright had worked on the design for a Unitarian Chapel at Sioux City for the architect, J. L. Silsbee, in 1887; see *Inland Architect,* 10 (June, 1887).

24. Wright, "In the Cause of Architecture," p. 164.

25. See Brooks, *The Prairie School,* pp. 80, 181; and Suzanne Ganschinietz, "William Drum-

mond,'' *Prairie School Review,* 6 (First and Second Quarters, 1969), 5–19.

26. Brooks, *The Prairie School,* pp. 79–80; and David T. Van Zanten, "The Early Work of Marion Mahony Griffin," *Prairie School Review,* 3 (Second Quarter, 1966), 5–16.

27. Brooks, *The Prairie School,* pp. 71 and *passim;* and James Birrell, *Walter Burley Griffin* (Queensland: University of Queensland Press, 1964).

28. Marion Mahony, *The Magic of America,* a manuscript, quoted in McCoy, "Rock Crest-Rock Glen," p. 16.

29. Brooks, *The Prairie School,* pp. 18–81 and *passim;* and Sally Anderson Chappell, "Barry Byrne, Architect: His Formative Years," *Prairie School Review,* 3 (Fourth Quarter, 1966), 5–23.

30. On the bank see Carl K. Bennett, "A Bank Built for Farmers: Louis Sullivan Designs a Building Which Marks a New Epoch in American Architecture," *Craftsman,* 15 (November, 1908), 176–85; Louis J. Millett, "The National Farmer's Bank of Owatonna, Minnesota," *Architectural Record,* 25 (January, 1909), 1–66; Paul E. Sprague, "The National Farmer's Bank, Owatonna, Minnesota," *Prairie School Review,* 4 (Second Quarter, 1967), 5–21; and David Gebhard, "Letter to the Editor," *Prairie School Review,* 4 (Third Quarter, 1967), 33–36.

31. Montgomery Schuyler, "The People's Savings Bank," *Architectural Record,* 31 (January, 1912), 48.

32. Ibid, p. 54.

33. Clipping, Cedar Rapids *Gazette,* date unknown. On Simmons see Wilhelm Miller, *The Prairie Spirit in Landscape Gardening* (Urbana: University of Illinois Press, 1915), p. 3; also see Leonard K. Eaton, *Landscape Artist in America, the Life and Work of Jens Jenson* (Chicago: University of Chicago Press, 1964).

34. Letter, Edward F. Winter to Richard Wilson, 29 January, 1975.

35. David Gebhard, "Louis Sullivan and George Grant Elmslie," *Journal of the Society of Architectural Historians,* 19 (1960), 62–68; and Gebhard, "William Gray Purcell and George Grant Elmslie and the Early Progressive Movement in American Architecture from 1900 to 1920" (unpublished Ph.D. dissertation, University of Minnesota, 1957).

36. This design was probably by Purcell since it is similar to his earlier Stewart Memorial Church, Minneapolis, 1909.

37. Researchers have disagreed over Elmslie's role, but Elmslie seems to have settled it; see letter from G. G. Elmslie to Frank Lloyd Wright, 12 June, 1936, reprinted in, *Journal of the Society of Architectural Historians,* 20 (October, 1961), 140–141. Also see: "A Sullivan Design That Is Not Sullivan's," *Western Architect,* 20 (August, 1914), 85; and Willard Connely, *Louis Sullivan* (New York: Horizon Press, 1960), 251–52, 257–59.

38. Benjamin Ricker (1868–1950), a native of Grinnell, possibly learned of the Prairie Style and Griffin through his wife's family who were natives of Oak Park, Illinois; *Grinnell Register,* 3 August, 1950. Ricker was apparently connected with E. W. Clark, Jr.'s subdivision. Clark was connected with the Merchant's National Bank as vice-president but he died 26 October, 1913, before Sullivan was contacted; *Grinnell Herald,* 28 October, 1913. The Clark Memorial Fountain was named for his father, Dr. (Senator) Elbert W. Clark (1842–1910), a prominent citizen.

39. This story is substantially repeated in Connely, *Sullivan,* pp. 260–61.

40. The scheme for many of Sullivan's banks, a large two-story volume of space, may well lie in the work of Frank Furness, a Philadelphia architect he worked for in 1873, and who designed a remarkable series of banks; see James F. O'Gorman, *The Architecture of Frank Furness* (Philadelphia: Philadelphia Museum of Art, 1973).

41. Brooks, *The Prairie School,* p. 292.

42. Brooks, *The Prairie School,* pp. 34–37; and J. William Rudd, "George W. Maher— Architect of the Prairie School," *Prairie School Review,* 1 (First Quarter, 1964), 5–11.

43. Brooks, *The Prairie School,* pp. 29–31.

44. The Dodd house plans, while dated 1910 after Elmslie had joined the firm, bear the imprint Purcell and Feick. They are initialed by Purcell who was certainly the designer. Purcell was the partner more interested in low-cost design, and the Dodd house is similar to his Charles A. Purcell house in River Forest, Illinois, 1909; illustrated in Brooks, *Prairie School,* p. 130.

45. "Vital Statistics and Professional Record of Wm. L. Steele, Architect. Omaha, Nebraska, September, 1941," in Purcell and Elmslie Collection, Northwest Architectural Archives, University of Minnesota, Minneapolis, Minnesota.

46. See his Davidson Building, 6th and Pierce Streets, 1913; and his Crane Company Warehouse, 3rd and Jackson Streets, *ca.* 1914.

47. Gebhard, "Purcell and Elmslie," p. 236.

See also William Gray Purcell, "John Norton, Mural Painter, 1874–1934," *Northwest Architect,* 18 (November–December, 1954), 14–16, 57–64.

48. The *Ladies' Home Journal* and *House Beautiful* were the most important; see note 18. In addition, *The Western Architect* of Minneapolis from December, 1911, onward published numerous articles and even devoted entire issues to the work of the Prairie School. Much of this material has been republished in H. Allen Brooks, ed., *Prairie School Architecture, Studies from "The Western Architect"* (Toronto: University of Toronto Press, 1975); The *Architectural Record* and the *Inland Architect,* participated to a lesser extent.

49. After 1925 the *Western Architect* with minor exceptions ignored the Prairie School. In 1910 *House Beautiful* moved to New York, and after 1914 ceased to support the Prairie School.

SECTION 2

1. C. E. Percival, "A House without a Servant," *House Beautiful,* 20 (August, 1906), 13–14.

2. William Morris, *Collected Works,* ed. May Morris (New York: Russell and Russell, 1966), XXII, 76.

3. "A Bachelor's Cottage in the Country," *House Beautiful,* 17 (April, 1905), 30.

4. Edgar I. Williams, "The Seashore House of Moderate Cost," *House Beautiful,* 70 (July, 1931), 26.

5. Frank Lloyd Wright, *The Living City* (New York: Horizon Press, 1958), pp. 102, 207.

6. Frank Lloyd Wright, *Buildings, Plans and Designs* (New York: Horizon Press, 1963).

7. "Our Cinderella's the Belle of the Block," *Better Homes and Gardens,* 20 *(November, 1941), 19*-21, and "Revived from Middle Age," *Better Homes and Gardens,* 21 (January, 1943), 24–25.

8. Frank Lloyd Wright, *The Living City* (New York: Horizon Press, 1958), p. 213.

9. Richard Pratt, "Opus 497," *Ladies' Home Journal,* 62 (June, 1945), 138–39.

10. Stan Fab Unit Bathroom by Standard Fabrication, Inc., advertised in *Everyday Art Quarterly* (Fall, 1947), No. 5 (Minneapolis: Walker Art Center), 25.

11. Bruce Brooks Pfeiffer, in conversation with Sidney K. Robinson, Taliesin, Spring Green, Wisconsin, August 7, 1975.

Catalogue of Prairie

School Architecture in Iowa

1. Algona, Henry C. Adams Building (Drugest Mutual Insurance Company), 123 East State Street. Sullivan, 1913–1914. *Sullivan was assisted in the design by Parker Berry who drew the rendering. The building was remodeled a few years ago by William Wagner, architect, of Des Moines.*

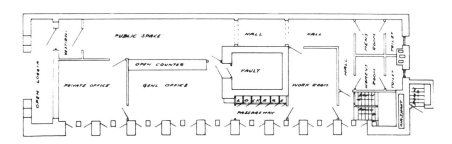

2. Cedar Rapids, Douglas B. Grant house, 3400 Adel Street, S.E. Wright, 1946–1951. *Designed on a 4-foot module, a 127-foot reinforced concrete roof shelters one of the most dramatically sited of Wright's Iowa houses. Limestone, quarried on the site by the Grants, is used for the walls and terraces.*

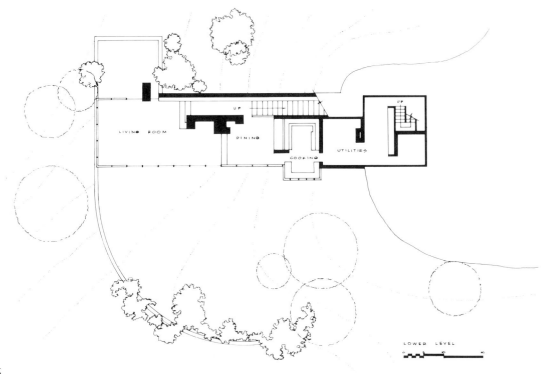

LOWER LEVEL

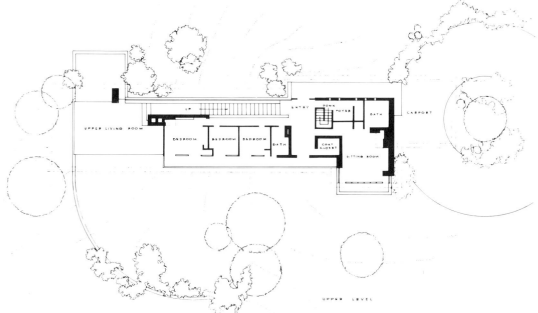

UPPER LEVEL

47

3. Cedar Rapids, The People's Savings Bank (Peoples Bank and Trust Company), 101 Third Avenue, S. W. Sullivan, 1909–1911. *A carefully articulated brick exterior encloses a magnificent banking space.*

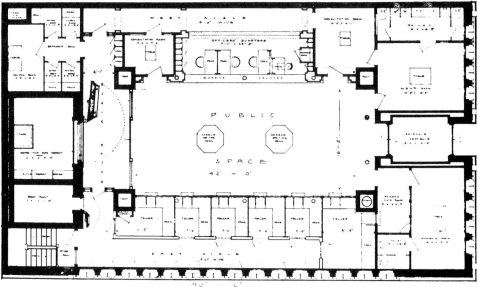

4. Cedar Rapids, Saint Paul's Methodist Episcopal Church (St. Paul's United Methodist Church), 1340 Third Avenue, S.E. Sullivan, plans revised by Jones and Elmslie, 1910–1914. *In spite of some rather heavyhanded revisions by Jones and the substitution of "stock" ornament, Sullivan's original conception of a great semicircular auditorium connected to the Sunday School and the social and office wings is preserved.*

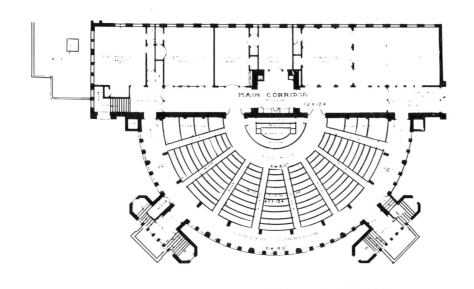

St Paul's M. E. Church : Cedar Rapids Iowa   Louis H. Sullivan
                                                                    Chicago

51

5. Cedar Rapids, Fred H. Shaver house, 2200 Linden Drive, S.E. Remodeling architect unknown; landscape architect Ossian C. Simmons, 1909–1911. *Long horizontal lines intersected by short verticals and an expansive interior space are used to create a local variation on the Prairie School style.*

6. Cedar Rapids, Vernon Heights Fire Station (Metro High School), 407 Seventeenth Street, S.E. Mayberry, 1912. *Certainly one of the most unusual variations on the Prairie School style, but rather heavily and clumsily handled.*

7. Charles City, George A. Blake house, 106 Blunt Street. Cleveland, 1914. *Has plans dated January, 1914–March, 1914.*

8. Charles City, A. B. C. Dodd house, 310 Third Avenue. Purcell and Elmslie, 1910–1911. *A budget house, differing from the standard builder's variety in its special trim and open interior plan.*

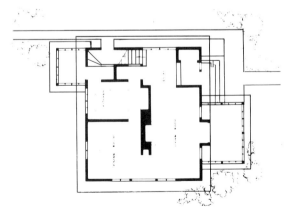

9. Charles City, Lindeman house, 104 Blunt Street. Cleveland, 1917.

10. Charles City, Alvin L. Miller house, 1107 Court Street. Wright, 1946–1951. *The cabinetry of this small Usonian house of stone, plaster, and cypress was made by Dr. Miller's son. Extensive site preparation in the form of retaining walls and terraces preceded the construction begun in 1951.*

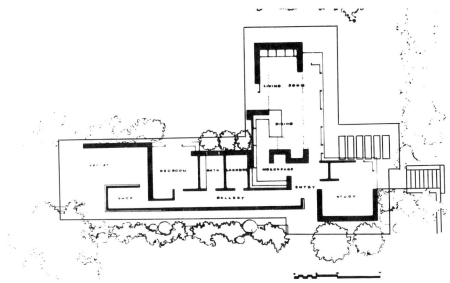

11. Clear Lake, E. V. Stillman house, 400 Seventh Avenue, North. Einar Broaten, 1917.

12. Clinton, Van Allen Store (Petersen Harned Von Maur Department Store), Fifth Avenue, South and Second Street. Sullivan, 1912–1915. *A structural steel frame and a thin skin covers the interior volumes.*

13. Des Moines, Dewey house, 305 Forty-second Street. Architect unknown, *ca.* 1915. *White stucco, overhanging eaves, articulation of piers and supports, and rectilinear treatment of the mass and details put this house within the Prairie School idiom.*

14. Des Moines, Gideon D. Ellyson house, 431 Twenty-eighth Street, Craftsman Bungalow Company, Inc., Seattle, Washington. Detailed by Proudfoot, Bird, and Rawson, Des Moines, 1914. *An example of how close the Bungalow idiom was to the Prairie School style. A frame building, cement stucco applied over metal lath.*

15. Des Moines, William H. Harwood house, 646 Forty-second Street. Architect unknown, 1907. *Harwood was the secretary-treasurer of Interstate Reality that laid out and developed this area of Des Moines. His house was a part of the development. It is remarkably similar to Wright's Winslow house, River Forest, Illinois, 1894, and also the work of George W. Maher.*

16. Dubuque, Eagle Point Park Shelters, Eagle Point Park. Alfred Caldwell, 1936–1937. *Caldwell had been a student of the landscape architect, Jens Jensen, and had been influenced by Wright's work. Erected with WPA funds, this complex is perhaps one of the most important and yet unknown examples of Prairie School work in the 1930s. Wendell Rettenberger, Caldwell's assistant, completed the project in 1937.*

17. Fairfield, Dr. James Frederic Clarke house, 500 South Main Street. Byrne assisted by Alfonso Iannelli on the interior, 1915. *Wright's early style is transposed by a former assistant into a personal style, the rectilinear forms cut by semicircular windows.*

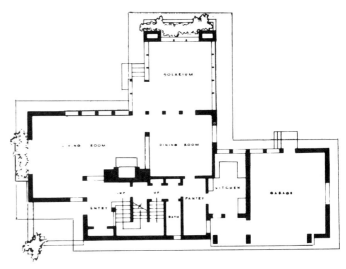

18. Grinnell, Merchants National Bank Building (Poweshiek County National Bank), 833 Fourth Avenue. Sullivan, 1913–1915. *A monumental scale is imparted to Main Street by the judicious use of ornament and careful adjustment of proportions.*

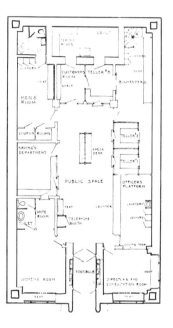

19. Grinnell, Benjamin K. Ricker house, 1510 Broad Street. Griffin, 1911; garage added by Byrne. *A solid brick box with emphasized corner piers that close the form and then intercut at the top for sleeping porches. On the interior the piers are hollowed out for book cases and cabinets. Tile work is by Marion Mahony.*

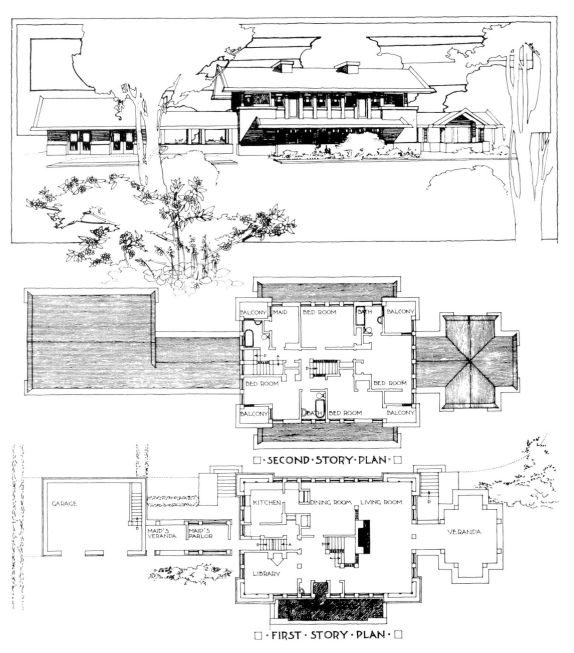

□ SECOND·STORY·PLAN·□

□ ·FIRST·STORY·PLAN·□

20. Grinnell, J. G. Shifflett house, 1327 Park Street. Cleveland, 1919. *A local variation on the Prairie School style.*

21. Hampton, Kohl house, 122 Fourth Street, S.C. Architect unknown, *ca.* 1920. *A small local variation on the Prairie School idiom, possibly by the Mason City architect, Einar Broaten.*

22. Iowa City, Jones House, 1155 Court Street. Architect unknown, *ca.* 1920.

23. Johnston, Paul Trier house, 6880 Northwest Beaver Drive. Wright, 1956–1959; north wing added by Taliesin Associated Architects, 1967. *Wright's last design in Iowa. As with most of the late works, John H. Howe carried out the design under Wright's direction.*

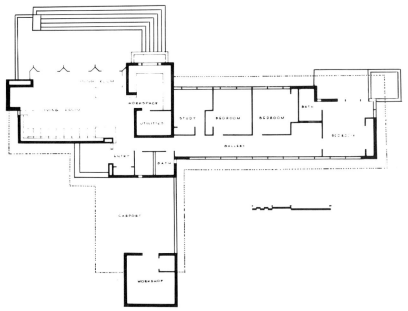

75

24. Keokuk, C. M. Rich house, 1229 Grand Avenue. Byrne, 1916. *Sited overlooking the Mississippi River, Byrne has combined certain uncommon features such as the projecting portico and the tile roof into a house that marks his movement away from the Prairie School idiom.*

25. Marshalltown, Church of Christ, Scientist, 500 West Main Street. Hugh Garden, 1902–1903. *The high vertical gables mark the building as apart from the Prairie School; however, the rectilinear nature of the trim and the excellent leaded glass windows executed by Giannini and Hilgart of Chicago mark it as typically within the Prairie School stylistic boundaries.*

77

26. Marshalltown, Robert H. Sunday house, Woodfield Road. Wright, 1955–1959; addition by John H. Howe, 1969–1970. *Howe was originally in charge of the design for this house whose generous scale owes something to previous concrete block houses and an exposition model house Wright set up in New York.*

27. Mason City, James C. Blythe house, 431 First Street, S.E. Griffin, 1913. *Rough-faced native limestone provides the base for a symmetrical composition of reinforced concrete. Even the garage is given a plate glass window to balance the block. Notable are the pre-Columbian motifs of the wall.*

81

28. Mason City, City National Bank Building and Hotel, West State Street at South Federal and South Enterprise. Wright, 1908–1910. *These buildings through their publication in the Wasmuth portfolio had a major impact on European architects after its publication in 1910. Sadly, this has not prevented them from being disfigured.*

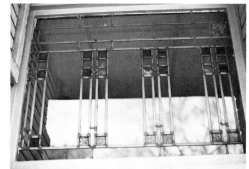

29. Mason City, Critelli house, 521 North Washington Avenue. Einar Broaten, *ca.* 1920. *Broaten's interpretation of Griffin's Melson design.*

30. Mason City, Samuel Davis Drake house, 28 South Carolina Street. Einar Broaten, 1914–1916. *Originally planned by Barry Byrne, the house was completely redesigned by Broaten. From the square block of the house, a solarium and garage project.*

31. Mason City, Carl F. Franke house, 320 First Street, S.E. Architect unknown, *ca. 1919. A deep, overhanging hipped roof was removed several years ago.*

32. Mason City, Edward N. Franke house, 507 East State Street. Byrne, 1915–1917. *Not as dramatic in massing as the other Rock Glen houses, still it has the typical characteristics of a low rising roof, limestone base, stucco upper walls, windows in banks, and crisp rectilinear forms.*

33. Mason City, Hugh Gilmore house, 511 East State Street. Byrne, 1915–1916. *A difficult site is masterfully handled by Byrne. His forms are more austere and simplified than those of Wright and Griffin. The house seems to nearly reverse itself, an unassuming scale on the street side, but from the rear it is revealed to be a large house. An addition has been made to the east over the dining wing.*

34. Mason City, Tom McNider house, 15 South Rock Glen. Curtis Besinger, 1959. *Wright's late style is used by a former Taliesin Fellow to integrate a more recent house in the development. Designed on a triangular grid, the house is fitted unobtrusively into a difficult narrow site. Cost prohibited the use of limestone and stucco as in the earlier houses so concrete block has been substituted.*

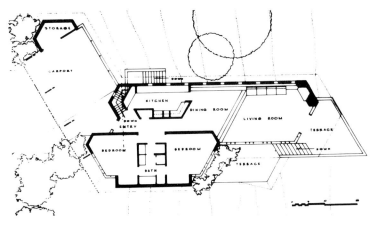

35. Mason City, Fred Lippert house, 521 North Washington. Fred Lippert, builder, *ca.* 1915. *Lippert was a well-known Mason City dweller. He constructed this house for himself on the other side of town from the Prairie School development. Einar Broaten may have been involved. Additionally, certain* Craftsman Magazine *characteristics are in this as well as other houses he built in the area.*

36. Mason City, Joshua Melson house, 56 River Heights Drive. Griffin, 1912. *Griffin's master stroke for the Rock Crest-Rock Glen development. Primeval in feeling, the house seems to grow from the cliffs.*

37. Mason City, Melson Mausoleum, Elmwood Cemetery. Byrne, 1915. *Constructed of native rough-faced ashlar similar to the Melson house, it is a simple and yet moving design.*

38. Mason City, Harry D. Page house, 21 South Rock Glen. Griffin, 1912. *Resting on a high, rough limestone base, the construction of the upper walls: reinforced concrete beams with an infill of stucco-covered hollow tile, is openly displayed. The curious round window for the basement is a Griffin trademark, dramatically contradicting the rectilinear character of the remainder of the design. A garage has been added.*

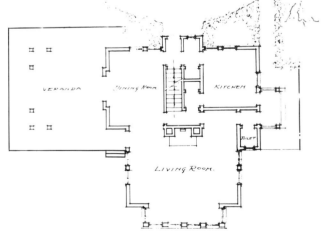

39. Mason City, George Romey house, 428 First Street, S.E. A. Felt, architect, 1919. *Located adjacent to the Rock Crest-Rock Glen community this house has certain Prairie School characteristics of blocky massing, projecting eaves, and abstract ornament. Felt is a virtually unknown architect supposedly with offices in Kansas City and Mason City.*

40. Mason City, Arthur Rule house, 11 South Rock Glen. Griffin, 1912. *Blocky and low, the house is nearly a cubical volume, with the corner piers emphasized and then denied by cutting away at the top for planters. Special note should be taken of the grouping of service and circulation facilities.*

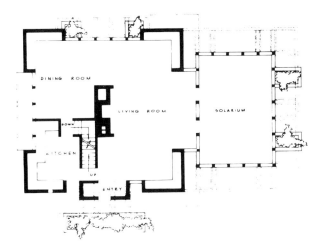

41. Mason City, Sam Schneider house, 525 East State Street. Griffin and Byrne, 1913–1916. *One of the most spatially inventive of the Mason City houses, one enters across a bridge from the street into a small entry hall off of which opens the dining room and, a half level lower, the living room. A massive fireplace divides the spaces. Later Byrne added bedrooms to either end of the house on the second floor.*

42. Mason City, Seaney house, 622 North Washington Avenue. S. Rivedal, builder; Einar Broaten, architect (?) *ca.* 1920. *Located on the other side of Mason City from the famous Prairie School development, the house illustrates a local builder's adaption of certain Prairie School characteristics, but greatly simplified for low-cost erection.*

43. Mason City, Dr. G. C. Stockman house, 311 First Street, S.E. Wright, 1908. *Wright's first work in Iowa, it is based on his 1906 scheme of "A Fireproof House for $5,000," except that here it is built with a wooden frame and stucco over lath.*

44. Mason City, Curtis Yelland house, 37 River Heights Drive. William Drummond, 1910–1911.

45. Newton, Bryant Denniston house, 1506 North Seventh Avenue, West. John (Jack) Howe, 1958–1961. *Designed by one of Wright's most talented assistants, it is on a 4-foot square grid with a central core containing fireplace, utilities, and kitchen.*

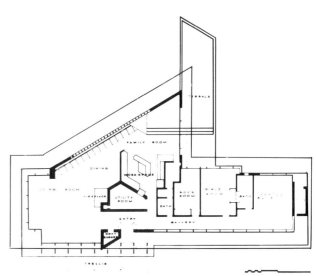

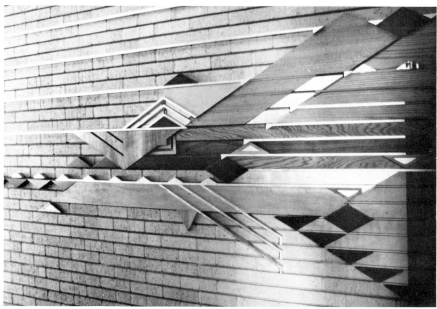

46. Oskaloosa, Carroll Alsop house, 1907 A Avenue, East. Wright, 1948–1951. *One of two Wright houses in Oskaloosa, the high ceiling of the gabled roof gives a spacious and stately character. Taliesin Fellow John deKoven Hill supervised construction.*

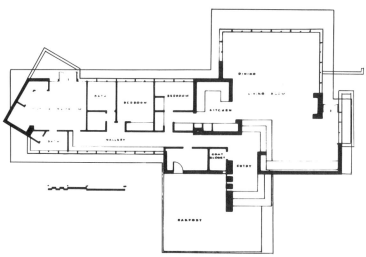

47. Oskaloosa, Jack Lamberson house, 511 North Park Avenue. Wright, 1948–1951. *Wright's only use of the triangular module in Iowa. Its exposed hilltop site precludes the usual extension of living area to a grade level terrace. Taliesin Fellow John deKoven Hill supervised construction.*

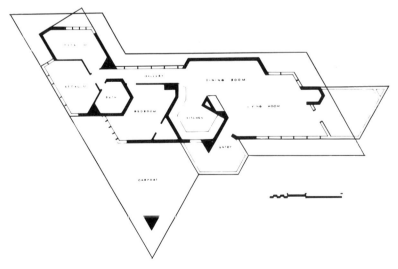

107

48. Ottumwa, Sacred Heart School, school wing addition, 119 Cooper Street. Byrne, 1959. *Much of Byrne's later work was confined to the Catholic Church. This is a simple addition of not very great importance.*

49. Quasqueton, Lowell Walter house and river pavilion, Wapsipinicon River. Wright, 1943–1948. *Supervised on construction by John deKoven Hill, a member of the Taliesin Fellowship. It is one of the most extensive design commissions Wright undertook in Iowa.*

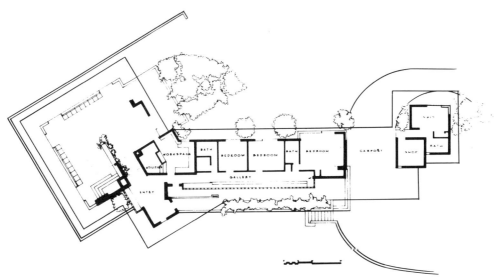

50. Sheffield, Henry Storck house, 1 Seventh Street. Architect unknown, *ca*. 1920. *A local variation that combines Prairie School characteristics with elements from the Craftsman idiom.*

51. Sioux City, Frank Albertson house, 3927 Country Club Boulevard. K. E. Westerlind of Colby and Westerlind, 1927. *This house is similar in many of its forms and details to Prairie School houses in Sioux City, by William Steele, for whom Westerlind worked for a period.*

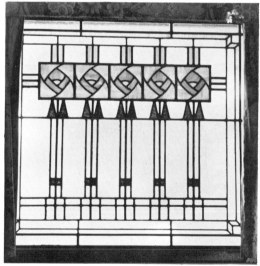

52. Sioux City, First Congregational Church (First Baptist Church). William Steele, 1918. *Beautiful and elegant elements such as the entrance are unfortunately marred by the awkward dome and round-headed windows.*

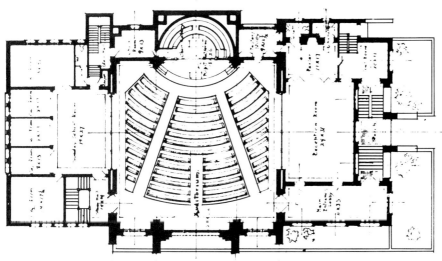

113

53. Sioux City, H. H. Everist house, 37 McDonald Drive. William Steele, 1916–1917.

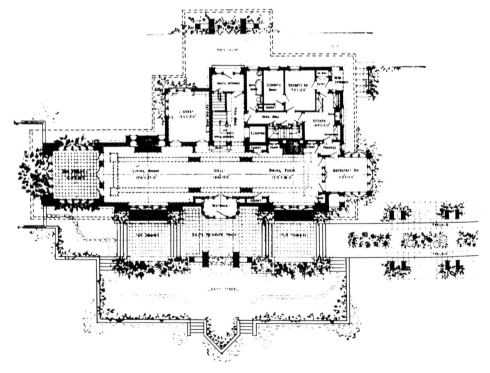

115

54. Sioux City, Knights of Columbus Hall (Sioux City Consistory Number Five), 8th Street and Douglas Street. William Steele, 1926.

55. Sioux City, Livestock National Bank (Northwestern National Bank) Exchange Building, Sioux City Stockyards. William Steele, *ca.* 1920. *An addition to the Exchange Building, Steele has used a lush Sullivanian type of ornament. Windows, the entrance and the interior have been severely altered.*

56. Sioux City, William Nystrom house, 605 Buckwalter Street. Curtis Besinger. *Designed by a former Taliesin Fellow (see Cat. 34). This house illustrates the merger of the Prairie School idiom into the contemporary ranch house vernacular.*

57–58. Sioux City, Sioux City Branch Libraries, Fairmont Park Branch (Greenville Community Center), 220 South Fairmont; Smith Villa Branch, 1509 George Street. William Steele, 1924–1927. *Identical twins, these were perhaps the last examples of the early Prairie School to be built in Iowa.*

59. Sioux City, Hafter Sve house, 2507 McDonald. William Steele, 1922. *Outside of the Prairie School idiom, the Sve house illustrates the application of Prairie School details to other idioms.*

60. Sioux City, Williges, 613 Pierce Street. William Steele, 1930–1931. *White terra-cotta with Sullivanian ornament used on the exterior.*

61. Sioux City, Woodbury County Courthouse, Seventh and Douglas streets. William Steele, architect; Purcell and Elmslie, associated architects; Alfonso Iannelli, sculptor; John Norton, muralist; Paul D. Cook, structural engineer; B. A. Broom, mechanical engineer, 1915–1918. *The high point of the Prairie School in both Iowa and the United States, the only major public building in the Prairie style.*

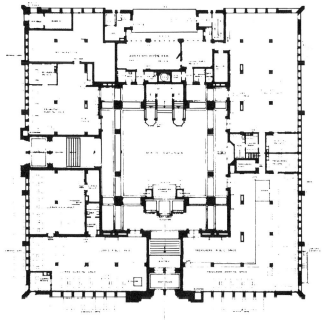

123

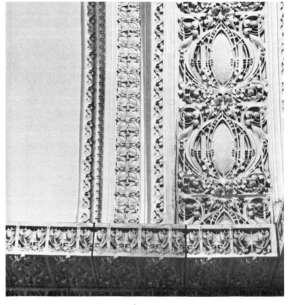

124

125

62. Waukon, J. H. Hager house, 17 Fourth Avenue, N.E. George Maher, 1913–1914. *Maher's designs are tighter, more formal, and contain certain eclectic elements that differ from the Wright works of the Prairie School.*

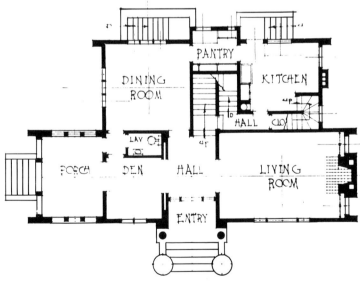

63. Waukon, O. J. Hager house, 402 Allamakee Avenue. Robert C. Spenser, Jr., 1907. *Departing from the normal stylistic idiom of the Prairie School, Spenser's design has English Arts and Crafts elements. Still the house in its simple and direct treatment of materials is related to the works of the other architects.*